DRINKING, FASTING, AND TATTOOS: SYRIAN WOMEN'S LIVED ISLAM

RELIGION AND INTERNATIONAL RELATIONS SERIES: 1

Series Editors: Jeffrey Haynes and A. Erdi Öztürk

Drinking, Fasting, and Tattoos: Syrian Women's Lived Islam

By Ozlem Ezer

First published in 2023 by Transnational Press London in the United Kingdom, 13 Stamford Place, Sale, M33 3BT, UK.
www.tplondon.com

Transnational Press London® and the logo and its affiliated brands are registered trademarks.

Requests for permission to reproduce material from this work should be sent to: sales@tplondon.com

ISBN: 978-1-80135-140-9 (Paperback)
ISBN: 978-1-80135-141-6 (Digital)

Cover Design: Nihal Yazgan
Cover Photo by Rostyslav Savchyn on unsplash.com

Transnational Press London Ltd. is a company registered in England and Wales No. 8771684.

DRINKING, FASTING, AND TATTOOS SYRIAN WOMEN'S LIVED ISLAM

Ozlem Ezer

TRANSNATIONAL PRESS LONDON

2023

CONTENTS

ABOUT THE AUTHOR

Ozlem Ezer studied English Language and Literature at Bogazici University in Istanbul, received her Ph.D. in Women's and Gender Studies at York University, Toronto. She completed her post-doctoral studies at Linkoping University, Sweden. Her first book Dogu, Batı ve Kadın (2012) was well received and has been taught in several literature programs in Turkey. Pausing full time teaching after 2015, Ezer focused more on engaged research, writing, and community work, especially with individuals who were displaced or deprived of financial and educational resources. She has reached out to several Syrian activists across Europe and North America and during her residency at CMES UC-Berkeley while working on her book on Syrian newcomers' transitions in several countries and delivered public lectures. She has been the recipient of funding from assorted international institutions, including DAAD, Joan B. Kroc Institute for Peace and Justice, the Lisbon Consortium, Swedish Research Institute, European Summer School in the Digital Humanities, International Women's Study Center in Santa Fe, Vrije University of Amsterdam, and Centre for Global Studies at Victoria University of British Columbia. In Athens and Amsterdam, she designed workshops and offered training on writing lives and how the practice can provide healing and agency.

ACKNOWLEDGEMENT

The only possible drawback of having a global circle of friends must be this very moment in front of the screen: the fear of missing someone whose contribution to this book is no less than any other's. Each one of them/you is unique and valuable, contributing to my efforts of giving back to this world despite its unexpected challenges. Without the thirteen women from Syria who shared their intimate thoughts and practices regarding their faith and Islam, this book wouldn't have come to life. I know there was more to say (always!) but the time and the circumstances led them to pause and even keep quiet at times. "Sex is easier to talk about than one's faith and religion," said more than one woman throughout the interviews (especially among feminist circles). Once the material is gathered and the research is completed, the writer needs to sit down, write, and edit several drafts, and for that, a quiet place to myself is the only way to completion. Nobody and nothing but me, the internet, and the computer (cats and coffee are allowed). It may sound selfish but essential to me in a world where women are expected to behave otherwise. I have been blessed with many homes that I don't own. The friends who own them share common traits: They are not driven by selfishness, the need to control others, or the desire to accumulate more. Their definition and practice of generosity is beyond most people's capacity to even imagine.

I have spent quality time in these houses, thinking, reading, writing, and cooking. Duff's Magic Home in San Francisco had a lot to offer especially this Spring (2022) as did the peace engineer Jerry McCann's conversations and unconditional support for anyone who needs it. He and Liz are generous souls, have I ever felt so welcomed for an extended period of time anywhere else? Teşekkürler to Necla Tschirgi for introducing us and more. Mary Ann and Ben Whitten's Heybeli-West in Pacific Grove and their excellent hospitality in the summer of 2021 contributed to this book's shaping. Mary Ann's gestures via Paypal with notes like "Happy Solstice!" always warmed my heart and the house too (literally!) My cousin Hâle Ikizler whose cute flat happens to be in the most convenient location for my "hectic Istanbul life" has been an amazing host. UmAy Home, the old family summer house near Istanbul became my writer's residency during the covid madness so I owe it to my family and to its new member Sevilya Sahutoglu whose presence in my life made this book and my sanity possible. What an amazing gift for someone who chose to stay child-free! The core Ezer family were unconditionally supportive even when figuring out what kind of book I was writing was not always clear, and this form of trust matters a lot! Jude Deason and Sallie Bingham of Santa Fe: Your wisdom, online availability, financial support, and solid encouragement for a like-minded next generation writer from Istanbul has been very memorable as we share the pains and madness of writing. Sema and Bülent Başol offered their home in Datça for the final stages of this book which saved me hours if not weeks due to its peace and quiet. What a gentle touch of support from a distance! Patricia Kubala, thanks for keeping your promise on keeping in touch. All academics whose works I came across online and needed badly for this book but didn't have access to. You entrusted your work to me as an email attachment generously whenever Esra Kazanbaş, the self-made woman and a dear colleague-in-progress couldn't find it at U of Toronto. Lindsy van Gelder for her personality, generosity, and entrusting her beautiful place in San Diego more than once. Special thanks to Fernando Enns and Zilka Spahić Šiljak for their encouragement as I was tipping my toes into the new waters of Theology and asking many questions as well as to the faculty at Vrije University who introduced me to the holistic and interdisciplinary framework of lived religion. The editorial team of Transnational Press London, thank you for your time, commitment and trust. And the ones who remain unnamed due to my bad memory and limited space: All the volunteers and guests of UmAy House who have been essential and complementary of each other and myself without even knowing it. Thank you so much to you all. Until the next time!

INTRODUCTION: LIVED RELIGION AND A CRITIQUE OF REFUGEE AND FORCED MIGRATION STUDIES

"Lived Islam is, like life itself, irremediably heterogeneous, unstable, dynamic, creative, and enriching. It is no longer possible to see it otherwise."

Kevin Reinhart[1]

The genesis of this book comes from a simple observation based on a rigorous and ongoing research since 2011: There is a major lack in literature regarding Syrian women's faith-based needs and practices in the field of Refugee and Forced Migration Studies (RFMS) and it stems from disciplinary tensions, hierarchies of knowledge, and missing multiple perspectives and positionalities in methodology designs. The lack affects the refugee assistance and resettlement projects negatively. Religion can be of significance for migrants and refugees for the following reasons: It can be the cause for the move, sustain people in difficult times, serve as an identity marker in new contexts, aid the displaced in giving meaning to their migration experiences, act as a source for reconciliation and healing, or help in resolving adjustment issues (Schreiter 2009, 157-168).

The meager debates in RFMS are limited to faith based organizations (FBOs), their policies, staff, and community feedback. The studies by Ezer (2019a; 2020), Dagtas (2018), Saunders et al. (2016), and Gozdziak (2008) are the only exceptions to my knowledge. The main reason for the lack of newcomers' narratives and perspectives, I suspect, stems from the dominance of Social Sciences in RFMS and disciplinary tensions which will be expanded later in the book. The research from the field demonstrates apologetic tones for subjective accounts and researchers' demands for measurable, empirical studies to validate them. The tensions in Social Sciences at large regarding the inclusion of Religious Studies have been fairly criticized by several scholars (Fountain and Lau 2013; Frederiks and Nagy 2016; Lauterbach 2014; Pargament 1997, 2006; Robbins 2006, 2016, Fadil 2019; Trinka 2019a). In this book, Religious Studies operate rather as a lens through which one can ask questions about women's life-on-the-move that have not been taken on board by mainstream Social Sciences or Cultural Studies. It demonstrates that religio-spirituality cannot be easily distinguished and separated from the flow of life even when certain

---

[1] Reinhart (2020).

individuals claim otherwise.

In fact, in their edited collection that bridges "Social science studies of migration" and "Religious Studies," Saunders et al. argue that scholars of religion "have focused not only on what migrants and members of the host society do in their religious practices, rituals, and organizations, but also on what they think and believe: the meanings and persuasiveness of their personal faith and religious teachings" (2016, ix). This statement is a recognition of a diverse and richly interwoven scholarship in Religious Studies over more "suspicious" Social Sciences (ix). Karen Lauterbach's diagnosis of "a missing dialogue" between anthropology and theology also points to a broader discomfort with managing religious language including religious experiences within Social Sciences (2014, 296). Ahmad and Reifeld also focus on how "the theological tradition differs from the view of the anthropologist" in the form of book view versus field view, but with some issues that I mention below (2017, xiv).

I propose lived religion as an epistemological and analytical tool which allows for interdisciplinarity while challenging hierarchical knowledge from multiple fronts. It serves as a bridge and an approachable way for ordinary people to take part in the dialogue among scholars and include non-academics in religio-spiritual knowledge making mechanisms. In Reinhart's metaphorical language, "Lived Religion is to theology what ordinary speech is to books of normative English grammar." In other words, it is similar to "colloquial speech" used in situations that do not require "particular linguistic care," and is "always locally inflected" like colloquial speech (2020, 33). Since the focus in this book is the Syrian Muslim women's lived religion, Reinhart's particular spotlight, that is, "lived Islam" serves well. What we both mean by lived Islam, is the Islam of ordinary Muslims, which exists not only in present but addresses the "actual or lived situation of Muslims at any time, in any place" (33). However, for sake of clarity and scholarly framing, the data here is a concentration of lived Islam by displaced migrant women from Syria.

The gender aspect in lived Islam informs the entire book. Indeed, I hope it inquires whether a new kind of gendered everyday Islam is emerging, one in which Muslim women claim agency, "not *in spite of* their everyday modes of living, but *through* their mastery of the minutiae of everyday life as part of a deeper ethical project of self-transformation." If some Syrian women believers seem to be followers, a major number mobilize themselves "as rational subjects to claim their own nuanced" and "unique ways of choosing to 'live Islam' in a taken-for-granted way in their everyday lives" (Liebelt and Werbner 2018, 7). Throughout my research, I came across only one special issue of an academic journal on the theme of gender and lived Islam (*Contemporary Levant* 2018). Each contribution is exceptionally valuable and timely, which will hopefully lead to other studies in near future.

Occasionally, one comes across recent studies on lived religion that use a sexist language (such as using the male pronoun/he in reference to anthropologist and theologian) and make overarching assumptions regarding the disciplines of Theology and Anthropology as in the Introduction of *Lived Islam in South Asia* (Ahmad and Reifeld 2017). Therefore, the gender aspect mentioned above is also a corrective of the studies that cannot be justified with any plausible argument. Furthermore, in its creating a space for fluid meanings and interpretations of Islam, this book will not be using statements such as "the antropologist faces the *problem* of grasping meanings which are fluid and interminate" (my emphasis, xiv) due to two main reasons: I consider fluidity not as a problem but a leeway especially when a study's aim is to build bridges. Secondly, I choose not to contribute to the binaries further by sharply distinguishing between an anthropologist and a theologian unlike Ahmad and Reifeld. On the contrary, fluidity is essential for producing non-hierarchical relationality and keeping porous lines among the stakeholders in research and writing.

The book title reflects the complexities of daily practices by some of these Syrian women whom I interviewed. Probably intriguing for readers from non-Muslim countries, for millions of others like myself who grew up in countries where fasting waiters during Ramadan serve alcoholic beverages at the restaurants in the touristic sections of their cities is part of life, the title is not as interesting. My uncle who stops drinking and smoking during Ramadan and celebrates its end by resuming both on the first day of the Eid was no stranger to the Syrians whom I met during my years of research and interviewing.

Most people in Turkey would still remember the murder of a barman, Oguz Atak, seemingly due to the provocation by the conservative media (TGRT channel) attacks about his tattoes, one of which was *Allah* in Arabic. The incident took place in 1997, but I still recall the heated discussions about it as the barman's boss -along with many of the victim's friends and family- told the press that Atak indeed had a deep faith in God, and always enjoyed conversations about Islam. It didn't surprise me that some of the Syrian women whom I interviewed had tattoos, some of which are made up of Arabic letters for *Allah*. Considering the gender-specific restrictions and taboos in Muslim majority countries, that women participants in this book kept their tattoes not as visible as the eccentric looking barman is understandable. Nevertheless, they shared with him the art of skin decoration and not-skin-deep faith.

The subtitle of the book is intentional and marks a distinction between "Syrian Women and Lived Islam" versus "Syrian Women's Lived Islam" in regard to methodology. Anna M. Gade's book *Muslim Environmentalisms* (2019) is examplary in this sense. She convincingly argues that the word "and" can be very telling as it contributes to a "reinvention of Islam as being a parameter" in sofar as Islam and anything (in my case, Syrian women, in her case, enviromentalisms so I will use the letter X for any imaginable topic) are set to "fit the constraints and expectations of what are often non-religious and non-Muslim" initiatives (37-38). Gade does not invalidate the uses of "Islam and X" but draws attention to the fact that such studies "have been produced primarily to support interests that may not originate with Muslims' own communities" (38). "Islam and X" approach is usually "imagined within a framework of plurality of religions, filtered through secular and essentially non-Muslim language," corresponding to "academic teaching in religious studies of world traditions overall" (38). Gade's criticism is backed up with several strong examples from the current literature not only in the introduction but throughout her book that she convinced me to choose "Syrian Women's Lived Islam" over "Syrian Women and Lived Islam." I also invite the readers to reconsider word choices, including the most conspicuous ones in a book, that is, the title.

In their discussion on the centrality of religion, Jung and Horstmann refer to earlier studies that religion serves as sanctuary and space of relief for the vulnerable, and they claim that it is more than a source of hope or break from suffering. Religion can be an integral part of refugees' space-making both public and private (home) in often hostile environments (2015). Similarly, Tobin argues that Islam in exile might become community-based and she shows how practices of place-making produce new forms of agency and learning, even under major political and economic distress (2020). Thus, re-territorializing the resilience-faith link and challenging the misleading or incomplete representations of refugees, women in particular, are also among the main driving forces behind this book. In-depth interviews over 90 hours of recording, followed by a regular follow-up process with 13 Syrian women in four countries between 2015-21 comprise the fieldwork data in the effort. Included is not only the wide-ranging literature review on lived religion and Islam but also a demonstration of how to begin assembling knowledges in ways that allow researchers think about meanings and purpose of our projects and subjects.

As Lauterbach points out, the role of religion in displacement situations "cannot be analyzed in depth" when a "mono-disciplinary approach" is adopted (2014, 292). Keller also argues that religious studies, sociology, and discourse research are thoroughly intertwined "possibly without fully realizing it" and draws attention to how religion played a major historical role in the emergence of sociology (2016, 320). Lena Gemzöe, Marja-Liisa Keinänen, and Avril Maddrell problematize a multiple-blindness among scholars of religion and gender, feminist theologians, scholars of gender, women, and feminist studies, and researchers in migration studies. They argue that despite the post-secular turn in the academy, the place of feminist studies of religion remains far from self-evident (2016, 20).

RFMS may claim to have an interdisciplinary approach by definition, however, the scholarship from Theology and Religious Studies are rarely used or recognized in it. This is an epistemological issue that points to a lack of communication among disciplines, which affects the refugee assistance and resettlement projects as well as policymaking during the massive displacement of the 21st century. In the humanitarian aid field for refugees, there is also a deep-seated prejudice against religion on the part of donor agencies and international NGOs (Zaman 2014). The majority do not want to engage with religiously motivated humanitarian actors even if it means not providing much-needed assistance to displaced communities, particularly inside Syria since 2011. Lack of knowledge about faith-based needs and practices of refugees remains a problem for the hosting governments, NGOs, human service providers, healthcare staff, and policy makers as much as the refugees themselves whose problems should be resolved through a holistic view.

Trinka's elucidating article "Migration and Internal Religious Pluralism" (2019a) is a major step in drawing links between migrants' lived religion and realities on the one hand, agencies and policies' traditional expressions on the other. He concludes that even though migrants spend a great deal of time in spaces of innovation and adaptation during their transition, the agencies they interact with represent the more traditional forms of the associated faith communities. Trinka argues that migrant religion is not conservative, as is often thought; rather, is marked by the same complexities and creativities of sedentary populations. Migration and religion have been and will remain central elements of the human experience, mutually influencing one another. My work aims to address and support his call for more and "badly needed" data about migrants' engagements with religion along their journeys (21).

Returning to the major lack in the field of RFMS regarding Syrian women's voices, their faith-based needs and practices: Even the extensive collection *The Oxford Handbook of Refugee and Forced Migration Studies* (2014) devotes only one chapter to discussing this issue. In it, Hollenbach reviews major religions' views of displacement and concludes that religion plays an ambivalent role in the process as it is simultaneously a cause of forced migration and an energizer for FBOs, faith-based organizations (447-459). Inspired by the work of Freire, Sink explains the difficulty of acknowledging refugee women's voices by their treatment as a separate entity rather than already a part of the community, which she relates to the larger structural issues in a society, the U.S. in her case (2017, 58). Another reason for the lack of refugee women's narratives, she argues, is the extensive amount of time required to establish the groundwork to receive those accounts, which I have not encountered in other studies, or considered it myself (41).

Furthermore, my book seeks to explore the specific questions of "What are some of Muslim Syrian women refugees' self-interpretive engagements with lived Islam, and in what ways (if at all) they contribute to adaptation and forming resilience in women's volatile states in a new country?" along with the sub-questions "How does displacement and loss affect refugees' faith-based practices and language during the resettlement process?", "Does renunciation or redefining a person's faith influence her coping mechanisms and resilience during and after the resettlement, and in what ways?"

The **introduction chapter** lays out the rationale of the book and draws links between newcomers' lived religion and realities while referring to the main resources in the field. I prioritize methodology as the **first chapter** of the book since I argue that any work about lived Islam of women-on-the-move need to be designed by a qualitative, collaborative, and combined methodologies. This is also where I situate myself into the study as a subject while discussing my possible biases and limitations that I was able to diagnose and share. A thorough justification of feminist research whether in Thelogy or Social Sciences is made in this chapter to demonstrate how the researcher and the researched engage in a complex process called research, particularly when listening to the survivors of atrocities in Syria is part of this process. The **second chapter** invites the reader for a clarification process where the terminology (religion, spirituality, religio-spirituality, lived religion, refugee, irregular migrant, newcomer, displaced person) is defined and tensions among different disciplines which lived Islam speaks to are presented. The first part of the **third chapter** is on literature review on representations and their critiques. It focuses on the latest debates on the depictions of refugees/newcomers before dwelling specifically on female newcomers' representations constructed with certain agendas, not necessarily to benefit them. The second part proposes lived religion both as an application for empowerment (resilience and personal growth are defined also in this section) and a tool to challenge the refugee stereotypes with an emphasis on agency. Examples are provided for how agency can be constructed in unlikely places. The **fourth chapter** closely relates to the previous chapter, an extention of it due to its content matter, that is, scholarship on Muslims in the English speaking academia, Muslim women in Europe and Muslim women refugees across different geographies. It reveals some problematic assumptions that have led to the current scholarship, such as churchification of Islam in Europe and other glitches that a researcher who plans to "study" Muslims might have. The inclusion of this extensive literature review contributes to both challenging and reconstructing representations that are discussed in the third chapter while revealing knowledge-making mechanisms and new debates on agency. **Chapter Five** recounts the interview process, introduces the profiles of 13 Syrian women, the interview selections with a focus on surviving displacement and trauma as well as how a lived Islam perspective works in their context. The complexities are reflected through the spirituality of the non-believers via lived Islam by using Orsi's concept of abundant events. **Chapter Six** revisits the various problematic perceptions of Muslim women, followed by several examples of rather unusually mixed faith practices of some of the Syrian respondents such as getting permanent tattoos and drinking while practicing Islam. First hand accounts by women and direct quotations from the interviews strengthen the key arguments in the book in a very accessible language for any reader who is interested in the subject. The **Conclusion** or Chapter Seven endorses the richer and thus the "messier" reflections of the data presented via the interviews, and it recommends further similar qualitative studies in Indonesia, post-Soviet countries, and Northern Cyprus. It also suggests integrating religio-spirituality into counseling and other displacement-induced services that are needed for an efficient and smoother resettlement of the newcomers who intend to construct a safer and stable life in their new countries via gender-sensitive lenses.

I hope that this book makes a significant contribution to the studies of lived religion, to the methodology of religion and migration, and to the research on religion-displacement nexus. It investigates the gender dimensions of displacement and presents Islam as a lived religion. While it serves as a valuable text for students and researchers in the mentioned fields, I also expect that the research speaks to a wide international readership due to its cross-cultural context.

CHAPTER I

METHODOLOGY EXPLAINED

Why Follow a Mixed, Qualitative, and Collaborative Path?

A nuanced way to view Islam as a lived religion is to observe and document what is performed and practiced by individuals in a specific framework (Syrian, women, displaced), and to study how these performances (including words and gestures) and practices inform their experiences

and meanings of Islam in everyday lives. On the journey, I have chosen the participative methodology, which is the product of a social constructivist understanding of knowledge and goes beyond dualisms (e.g., researcher/researched). In-depth interviews, self-reflexivity, liminality of the researcher/practitioner, narrative analysis (meaning-making and relationality being in its core), and awareness of positionality and relational self will be discussed in this section in regard to and with examples of participative methodology. My methodology also corresponds to what Ghorashi calls "narrative engaged research" where participants can position themselves within discursive spaces and contribute to the research through engagement at the boundaries of theory and practice (2021, 49-50). Such mixed methodologies are particularly significant "for refugees specifically and even more so for refugee women, who are not used to taking up space and at times" (49) because of their past experiences as Ghorashi argued elsewhere (2008).

Qualitative methods such as interviews are favored by social constructivist approaches because they take a greater account of the porous line between the researcher and the researched. The overall effect that I plan to achieve via this mixed method approach is an engaged scholarship where the contributors feel empowered by agreeing to participate and become part of a wider and collective advocacy if they choose to. It is a research *with* and *for*, rather than *on*, participants. In narrative methods, people recount stories to help them organize and make sense of their lives; thus, their accounts become more functional and purposeful. Building and maintaining a non-hierarchical relationality is another key component in my work.

I am unconvinced that the lack of literature in "Religio-Spirituality and Migration Studies" is due to the "serious social scientists who dismissed the idea that religion could be *scientifically* measured" (Dillon and Wink 2007, 214 *emphasis* mine). My skepticism extends to the ones that were conducted especially on Muslim's religiosity due to the notion that church-attendance is incompatible to mosque attendance as a criterion when it comes measuring Muslims' religiosity (Dasti 2014; Olufadi 2016; Salam, Muhamad, Leong 2019). McAndrew, Siobhan and Voas' article is an exception in acknowledging difficulties with measuring and interpreting religiosity (2011). I remain suspicious of the works including some massive longitudinal undertakings such as Dillon and Wink's *In the Course of a Lifetime* (2007). Not dismissing but questioning the studies whose argument revolve around the scientific measurability of spirituality (de Jager Meezenbroek et al. 2012) and religiousness is part of this book as the selected methods demonstrate.

I also borrow methods from oral history, feminist standpoint as well as literature review on resilience and coping with trauma (Geiger 1990; Hogue 2006; Pargament 1997; 2006; Sprague 2005; Neitz 2011; Laban 2015; Eghedamian 2017; Trinka 2019; Hoffman 2020; Alfani 2021; Kanal and Rottmann 2021). I hope that this study will trigger new debates on integrating religio-spirituality into counseling and other services that are available and/or needed for an efficient resettlement for the displaced individuals who intend to build a safer life in their new countries.

As there is still no commonly accepted set of epistemological and ontological premises regarding the use of lived religion as a theoretical framework, lived religion is better described as a methodological approach rather than as a theoretical scaffolding. In this study, lived religion also serves as an epistemological and analytical tool which welcomes interdisciplinarity. However, significant theorizing efforts are flourishing as the special issue of *Journal of Contemporary Religion* demonstrates (Knibbe and Kupari 2020). The editors pinpoint lived religion's seminal influences including theories of the everyday, embodiment theory, phenomenological anthropology, theories of practice, and feminist theory (164). The lived religion approach abandons macro-level questions and attempts at theorizing the future of religion in modernity by focusing on how religion is practiced. The assumption of an "inherent incompatibility between religion and modernity" is discarded, and instead, it investigates how religion is experienced (159).

The primary focus of lived religion is on diverse beliefs and practices, not on reflections. Experts such as prophets, priests, imams, theologians, and their organizations are not the sole authorities and foci of interest. In fact, it is rather the lay people. "Lived religion" thus shifts the focus in order to attend to the religiosity of individuals and groups as embedded in the contexts of biographies, which implies that the phenomenon in question doesn't have to have an overtly religious nature (Streib et al. 2008, ix-x). The concept of lived religion enables me to reframe traumatic events such as war and displacement in the case of Syrian refugees' experiences, especially because these occurrences demand immediate reconfigurations when authorities spread conflicting messages, or are not available.

Unlike some universal *sui generis* macro-level definitions of religion, lived religion attempts at "theorizing the future of religion in modernity by focusing on how religion is practiced" (Streib et al. 2008, 158). Lived religion gives priority to devising research strategies that employ ethnographic and historiographic methods to show how religion is shaped through innumerous habits, daily practices, and patterns of social life. Via lived religion, the possibility of a non-reductionist understanding of people's engagement with the supernatural can be explored. For instance, Knibbe shows possibilities of being both non-reductionist and critical of the religious worlds when one engages in research on lived religion (2020). Her aim is to approach religion as performed and materialized without reducing religious practices to psychological, social or cognitive functions. She boldly tackles the moments of tension between academic worldviews and one's own moral orientations and values while theorizing them.

Theorists of lived religion commonly identify the terms "popular religion" and "vernacular religion" in their scholarly categorizations but they work towards validating lived religion over them. All religious phenomena, that is, practices, rituals, beliefs, values, norms, doctrines, objects can be studied as lived religion. I am aware that one needs to constantly reflect on the scope of lived religion scholarship and stay alert to possible omissions. Paying attention to the margins has been a crucial objective in the study of lived religion, and this book articulates some of the female voices that have been temporarily pushed into the margins.

Having stated that, one should not get the impression that the religion of dominant groups is excluded as a legitimate area of enquiry within a lived religion approach. In other words, "focusing solely on the disadvantaged is untenable as it gives the impression that 'élite' religiosity does not fit in the category of lived religion and is somehow fundamentally different," clarify Knibbe and Kupari, which would be contradictory to the inclusivity of the approach. The lived religion will remain "porous as well as pragmatic," taking up methods, theories, and concepts developed in sociology, anthropology, religious studies, theology, history, philosophy, and feminism (Knibbe and Kupari 2020, 167-68).

The starting point for a lived religion approach takes in religious practices and its varied expressions, namely, "what people actually do, experience, desire, hope, think, imagine, and touch" in daily contexts (Ganzevoort and

Sremac 2017, 5). This opens the path for exploring its overlapping elements with feminist and narrative methodologies in my study. For instance, the statement that emphasizes individuals' navigation "in a continuous negotiation with their personal and social context and narrative" (Sremac and Ganzevoort 2018, 3) is compatible with and complementary to "personal is political," a major pillar of feminist thought. In other words, women should not hesitate to create spaces for relentless negotiations through the power dynamics in their private and public circles. In addition, lived religion's embeddedness in the context of biographies renders an organic quality to this book due to its use of selected life stories of Syrian women raised as Muslims.

Mary Jo Neitz's article on feminist methodologies is pertinent here due to her proposal on appropriating methods as a means to women's empowerment, which has been a driving force for my work. In connection to theology, Neitz mentions ways of which scholars of religion can conduct research from the feminist standpoint (FS) of the disadvantaged (2011, 56). Feminist standpoint epistemologies underline the importance of recognizing that knowledge is always developed as a "view from somewhere" thus privileging certain modes of knowing over others (Haraway 1988; Woodhead 2013, 12). Among the three positions in feminist research (feminist empiricism, standpoint and radical construction), Neitz focuses on feminist standpoint (FS) for several reasons which also resonate here (61).

First, FS built a tradition of its own for studying religions that are outside of the majority or dominant culture. This includes faith-based practices of less-powerful groups such as displaced individuals in any society. Second, FS epistemology asserts that all knowledge is partial and located, and FS analysis speaks about intersectional matrices of oppression in the production of all knowledge (Neitz 2011, 54). In this book, FS corresponds to bringing out authentic voices of a disadvantaged community, namely the Syrian female survivors of war and displacement in a context of faith-based engagements. A more recent development in FS is the study of the lived experience of ordinary people, which indicates a shift in attention towards the embodied practices of ordinary individuals (61). I connect FS to the concept of "lived religion" (Sremac and Jindra 2020; Sremac and Ganzevoort 2018; Ganzevoort 2014) and explore it further in the context of Syrian refugee women's religio-spiritual lives.[2]

Refugee/newcomer women by definition occupy in-between spaces, constantly negotiating a sense of selfhood, an identity that is different from

---

[2] Sahur/suhur is the meal consumed early in the morning by Muslims before fasting (sawm) before dawn.

their families in Syria and from the host-country identity at large. Their struggle in and with Islam as taught in Syria offers a rich site for theorizing, but requires an equally fluid conceptual framework to investigate the empirical material. This point is our challenge as researchers in inter/trans disciplinary studies whose work space may not be as fluid as the displaced, something we need to keep in mind.

Gemzöe and Keinänen warn against a simplistic attitude in the attempts of integrating the study of religion to gender studies, and argue that it should go beyond the mere adding of another identity marker to the mix of an intersectional analysis (2016, 3). Dominant approach in Western feminist studies is intersectionality but the term is not used out of an academic decorum *per se*. My attempt here is to readdress the relationship between feminist studies and studies of Islam as lived religion by linking different theoretical veins for the evolution of both fields. Intersectionality is embedded in and informs the whole study.

Exercising Self-Reflexivity: Biases, Limitations, and Recommendations

My previous work with Syrian women refugees between 2015 and 2019 highlighted several theme-based issues, demonstrating a potential to grow beyond biographical accounts. Among them were the links between displaced individuals' developing and maintaining resilience through faith-based practices and whether disowning, embracing or rearticulating one's faith influences her coping mechanisms during and after the resettlement (Ezer 2019a). Providing space for unheard women refugees' voices from Syria in mainstream knowledge production channels and venues has been my priority.

My first bias was that the believers of faith systems might be better equipped to overcome trauma as refugees, experience a deeper understanding of life's purpose, and develop better awareness of personal strengths (Acquaye et al. 2018; López et al. 2015). That is why powerful agnostic-atheist Syrian women (who use the terms interchangeably) are included in the interviews. Religious beliefs may infuse tragedy with meaning, and there are cases in which displaced individuals make sense of their exile through their religion (Mayer 2007). However, this has not always been the case and caution is needed in such claims.

My second bias relates to knowledge making mechanisms and borders of academic disciplines. I have been critical of Social Sciences whose language mirrored science for validity so I used to prioritize Humanities due to their ancient and enduring existence in history. Social Sciences were established very recently -mostly in the 19th century- and have claimed to produce "scientific studies" on human psyche and body. Recent works with interdisciplinary approaches in which neuroscientific and clinical perspectives are merged into Social Sciences helped me overcome this bias (Koss-Chioino and Hefner 2006). I noticed that the scholars and practitioners in several fields of Social Sciences have been exposing and criticizing their own (outdated) methods and language use as well, especially when informed by feminist and postcolonial studies after the 1970s. The sociologist Meredith McGuire's works present strong yet constructive criticism of her discipline which helped expand the scope of my research (2008; 2006; 2002).

I am also convinced that reflections upon one's own history and personality during research and writing process can add depth to understanding of one's academic work (Sleep 2000). The self-reflections keep me alert and serve positively in my development as a researcher of gender and religion. When I reflect on the process of the research, three voices can be identified: the critical academic, the personally inflected listener, and the writer who has been working on this book. Negotiations and interactions among these voices have been challenging at times since their roles and priorities on what and how much to include don't necessarily overlap.

Moreover, underlining biographical reflection connects to the above-mentioned nature of knowledge production (Haraway 1990) and acknowledges the experience of the researcher and its influence on the research process. Ruokonen-Engler and Siouti consider reflections of subjective experience as a productive method for doing research in transnational settings. In fact, they endorse biographical reflexivity as a necessary methodological tool in research practice (2014, 251). I consider Susan Ossman's work as exemplary practices of merging different voices that appear throughout the research process, including the voice of an artist (2021; 2013).

For some scholars who are deeply rooted in a monodisciplinary manner, a possible criticism if not limitation might be that the theoretical framework of lived religion is considered "still too much in its youth" (Ammerman 2014a, 204). However, the body of knowledge grows, along with new keywords and concepts. Lived religion is inherently grounded in "detail and diversity which only ethnographic work can fully apprehend" (204). Its novelty as an approach isn't necessarily a limitation since its roots can be traced back to Charlotte Perkins Gilman and W. E. B. Du Bois (192). However, I share Ammerman's concerns that lived religion scholars may suffer from negotiations in the current assessment-based academic settings. On a positive note, shared methods will allow potential bridges among history, anthropology, religious studies, sociology, and psychology (203). As briefly mentioned in the methodology section, theorizing efforts have been in progress (Knibbe and Kupari 2020). The editors include theories of the everyday, phenomenological anthropology, theories of practice, and feminist theory in their list of lived religion's formative influences (164). Anczyk and Grzymała-Moszczyńska also propose bridging disciplines -particularly of psychology and religious studies- as "a win-win situation" and advocate a cultural approach to achieve it (2020, 29).

Finally, my interviews were conducted in English (except the one with Lutfia) so the need for gathering data from the women refugees with no English remains as much as the need for culturally sensitive and faith-literate female interpreters. Moreover, I only utilized resources in English for the literature review, which poses a limitation to my research. Paradoxical as it may sound, that limiting the language to English enabled me and the participants for building longer and deeper personal connections throughout and after the interviews is worth mentioning. They were more engaged and collaborative whenever *they* wanted to be. Besides, the women had access to their narratives that I composed and were able to comment on and edit before the publishing team. English as the *lingua franca* of our time is a double-sword due to its simultaneous inclusion and exclusion in many contexts, and Religious Studies and RFMS are no exceptions.

Writing the Self, Using the Self: Auto/Biography Method in Lived Religion

When I engage in sensitive, potentially painful topics, the dilemmas of human frailty and struggle, I acknowledge that the outcome or the narrative of any self involves others too, thus relationality. Thus, the writing of the self raises ethical issues that go beyond the protocols and procedures of ethical committees. Davies argues for a strong critical awareness since the writing of the self can lead to self-absorption and a breaking down of the boundaries between author and the text, which leads to the research becoming simply about itself (2008, 9). However, a genuine reflexivity, which shares the researcher's journey, self-questioning and dilemmas in the research process, brings the research and its methodology to life, Berry contends, and shows how the researcher herself develops and is vulnerable within the process (2018, 208).

According to Berry, the self that is constructed in feminist theological research is a particular and situated self; it is distinct from the self of journals and diaries, home and family, of intimate and even professional relationships (205). Ngunjiri, Hernandez, and Chang argue that "research is an extension of researchers' lives," and although most social scientists' training condition them to "guard against subjectivity and to separate self from research activities, it is an impossible task" (2010, 2). Scholarship is inextricably connected to self in the plural form. These selves may "overlap, interact and collide but always there is an element of mediation, of storytelling" (Berry 2018, 205). Mediation is embedded in relationality.

Reflexivity makes clear that research is a relational process. Orsi's Sartrean approach to research in general (2005) is one that particularly resonates with me: "Research is a relationship" between human beings, Sartre wrote in 1968, "and the relationship itself must be interpreted as a moment of this history" (qtd. in Orsi 2005, 174). "Things happen in the course of conversation," Orsi continues in his formulation of humanistic approach, that "emotions are generated, fantasies provoked" as both the researcher and the researched create and recreate each other. In this complex process of research, a critical awareness is necessary to monitor and study the process (175).

The researcher's personal involvement with the topic is seldom made explicit and visible. In transnational migration theory, the justification of why the researcher undertakes her work and how this is linked with transnational knowledge production remains invisible (Köngeter 2012). However, it is reflected in "neighboring disciplinary discourses, for example in interdisciplinary gender studies, cultural anthropology and post-colonial approaches" (Ruokonen-Engler and Siouti 2014, 252). They argue for reflecting on one's biographical experience as part of "an interactive research process in which embodied biographical knowledge is brought into dialogue with a multivocality of theories" which this book allows the space for (254).

Reflexivity and agency can be related in research. "Strong reflexivity" in the way Harding used is about seeing individuals in relation to each other via their situatedness in particular histories and communities, which includes the researcher herself (1993, 70-71). These "positioning practices" (see Alvesson, Hardy and Harley, 2008) can lead to creating a potential to divert from "the dominant hierarchical categorisations of self and other" and make room for agency (Ghorashi 2021, 53).

That I was born and raised in Turkey until college graduation, and have been acquainted with and exposed to the similar cultural and religious conditions of Syrian women facilitated my interviews. I grew up in a middle-class urban family in Istanbul. After a relatively liberal college life within the safe walls of a university that was originally founded by Americans in the

19th century, I left to study abroad. I was naturalized as a U.S. citizen in 2006 and had to go through intensive paperwork and security checks prior and throughout the process. As a young woman with a Turkish passport who traveled in Europe, various forms of frustrations and degradations are in my baggage of mobility history. I have encountered discrimination and outrageously stereotypical questions about my culture and religion for decades. I fit Ossman's definition of a serial migrant, that is, a person who has lived in several countries (Canada, Germany, Sweden, Greece, Turkey, the US), calling each one at some point home (2013). Similar to some of Ghorashi's research, I too was able to experience and check with the Syrian participants about this "balancing act of sameness and difference" that emerged through sharing stories, which created "unusual connections through confusion, surprise, imagination and self-reflection" for both sides (2021, 54). That Syrian women might have perceived my interviewer position as more relatable than other female researchers who work on similar topics and approached them for collecting data is plausible and definitely no coincidence.

I reject a dualism that sees the material less worthy than the spiritual, and instead affirm a holistic view of body, emotion and spirit in an integrated whole. Acknowledging the use of our selves in research is to deny the dualistic compartmentalism that separates out academic research as a category that is separate from the rest of life. Feminist theological research is an embodied, emotional, intellectual, and spiritual journey. On my path, being hosted by the newcomers, feeling at home in their temporary makeshift dwellings, and integrating their work into mine (e.g., receiving Arabic translation services for my project's website, asking for help to design the cover of my book where their stories featured) are some examples of rejecting dualistic compartmentalism.

Behar's statement that "writing vulnerably takes as much skill, nuance and willingness to follow through on all the ramifications of a complicated idea as does writing invulnerably and distantly" has led me to integrate a minimum amount of personal and vulnerable experiences in this book (1996, 13). However, I shared some of them with the Syrian interlocutors not only for building relationality but also for releasing certain frustrations regarding the mistranslation of Islamic practices and gender prejudices in the Global North. Sharing didn't make me feel vulnerable or unprofessional, in fact, quite the opposite. In this regard, I practiced self-reflexivity mostly in conversations also with colleagues who are involved in similar situations or in an irregularly kept diary.

Many researchers decide on a topic that resonates with their own experience in some way or another, and the process of hearing, recording, reflecting on and interpreting others' stories can become a way of making sense and meaning out of certain perplexing experiences. Walton suggests that the reflexive element can be therapeutic (2014, xxix). While acknowledging that she did not take this risk until well-established in her career, Etherington writes of her own personal and reflective writing that it "has changed my sense of the experiences I have written about and strengthened me in the process" (2004, 142). Trin Minh-ha with whom I had the opportunity to converse in her UC Berkeley office told me that she received 35 rejections from publishers for *Woman, Native, Other* (1989), her groundbreaking work which affirms the power of women's narratives. Having been recognized and praised in the academia after a relentless struggle and patience, she still continues voicing other women intertwined with her own along the road as in *Elsewhere, Within Here: Immigration, Refugeeism and the Boundary Event* (2011). She has persisted in writing and recommends it to all BIPOCs.

Orsi's language to express his criticism of distanciation of the researcher is strong, yet would sound completely familiar to most scholars as we tend to:

> tame what is wild and threatening and dangerous specifically to us because of the details of our particular childhoods about different forms of religious experience and practice. This is what makes so much religious scholarship dull and beside the point. It is also the reason why scholars of religion spend so much time in making sterile taxonomies, gridding what we study into safe -and discrete-categories. These various complex anxieties, needs, and discomforts constitute the existential difficulties of fieldwork in one's own religious tradition. (2005, 161)

Combined with these anxieties, needs, and discomforts of conducting fieldwork in one's religious tradition is the publishers' reluctance to accept alternative writing where the scholar/researcher is present as in the experiences of Etherington and Trinh Minh-ha. Behar's statement on writing vulnerably presents a mammoth of challenges that are convincing for me to use self-reflexivity cautiously. I managed to experiment with it elsewhere and may continue to do so in future (Ezer 2011; 2015; 2017a; 2017b; 2019b). The therapeutic effect that Walton mentioned can be created on extratextual platforms and still proves to be healing.

Within Religious Studies, life story accounts and biographical research are considered very useful methods since people's beliefs are diverse and multifaceted, which can be harder to identify in quantitative studies. For instance, Bremborg's interviews led her to gain insight into people's religious lives that former studies of organized religion had not revealed (2011, 310-12). In *Lived Religion*, McGuire also shares that people's religion was much more complicated than she had thought during the early stages of her research; in fact, "ever changing, multifaceted, often messy, even contradictory" (2008, 4). Oral History interviews result in rich, complex, and nuanced data also in undertaking studies on women survivors of atrocities and obtaining difficult knowledge (Leydesdorff 2014; Sheftel 2018; Spahić Šiljak 2014). An earlier study also appropriated life story interviewing in its attempt to capture female, feminist, and Muslim identities of the interviewed women and stands in evidence to the effectiveness of this method in interdisciplinary studies (Spahić Šiljak 2012).

Life stories can provide an integrative ground for bridging Humanities to other disciplines such as Medicine, particularly to the areas of mental health and therapy due to their usefulness in eliciting accounts of suffering (as segments of life narratives) in clinical encounters. Consequently, they have the potential to act as "therapeutic tools" which might serve refugee mental health providers (Gozdziak 2004, 208). A consistent feedback that I received throughout and after the interviews from the interlocutors was of appreciation, and the respondents mentioned that narrating and reflecting on one's life was a pleasant and profound experience.

Biographical research methodology (Ruokonen-Engler and Siouti 2014) also enables both the researchers' and refugee women's experiences and activities as individuals while they move in their daily lives between different realms of operation, such as locally rooted family life and transnational networking. In the field of transnational migration studies, the biographical approach is particularly well suited to empirical investigations of transnational migration processes because it offers a way of reconstructing diversity and complexity. The transformational character of migration phenomena is revealed efficiently through biographical narration and analysis. According to Ruokonen-Engler and Siouti, biographical research provides "an appropriate and analytically rich way to make theoretical sense of changing social phenomena in the age of globalization," making reconstructing social change and its influence on biographical subjects possible (251).

Marjo Buitelaar also offers inspirational directions in lived religion by mobilizing a dialogical approach and intersectionality. She argues that the dialogical nature of storytelling helped her to "appropriate elements from the Islamic grand narrative" (that is, the hajj/pilgrimage in her work) and mix them with "the vocabulary from the discourse about the authentic self," thus producing multi-voiced accounts (2020, 9). Halleh Ghorashi is another social scientist who used "dialogical narratives" in her work with women refugees multiple times since 2008. The methodological assumption she adopts is that "by connecting academic, professional and personal knowledge, various levels of reflection will emerge to unsettle the normalised images of the self and the other" (2021, 50). Connecting the multiplicity of non-academic positions through dialogical narratives with academic knowledge enabled Ghorashi "to co-create knowledge within which the processes of data collection and analysis were partially merged" (50).

Engaging with the narratives of refugees and refugee-related professionals, the research process involved writing life stories of women with different backgrounds and sharing them. The team later analyzed the narratives with the participants so that the refugee participants were able engage in the process of analysis of their narratives. This collaborative analysis eventually led the narrators to reclaim their past in an empowering manner, providing a much-needed agency for the refugees and an awareness -if not an eureka moment- for the refugee-related native Dutch professionals on the negative impact of normalizing discourse in the governing system. My research is in line with Ghorashi's methodology as I have witnessed the power of sharing narratives and consider it as one of the significant engaged forms of scholarship and a way to think about power and agency.

CHAPTER II

LIVED RELIGION AS A POTENTIAL RECUPERATOR OF MULTIPLE TENSIONS

Gender, Women, and Feminist Studies (GWFS), Religious Studies, Theology, and Migration Studies

This chapter will point to some debated borders, missing links, and lacunae across the following disciplines: Religious Studies, Theology, life story accounts and biographical research (Qualitative methodologies in Social Sciences), Gender, Women, and Feminist Studies (GWFS), and Migration Studies. My aim is not to reiterate or further complicate the current arguments, however, a summary will orient the readers to contemplate where they and this book stand on academic mappings. A study by Elina Vuola (2016) captures these "mutual challenges" exquisitely and serves as an informative eye-opener for me as a scholar of GWFS who conducted ethnographic fieldwork as well as oral history interviews for the past ten years.

My official engagement with Religious Studies began in Fall 2018 and is still ongoing as of 2022. Vuola, with a previous extensive criticism on women's religion and intersectionality (2012), contends that feminist theorizing has "often been blind to and sometimes openly negative toward any positive synergy between feminism and religion" (2016, 317-18). As a staunch proponent of intersectionality in research, Vuola's statement that "even theories of intersectionality, which explicitly pay (self)critical attention to the blind spots of feminist theory" have been "unable to see religion as an important factor in women's lives" was disappointing for me to say the least (2012, 141). Feminist theologians, she argues, have the knowledge and the skills to "de- and re-construct" religions "from within the tradition," that is, to "critique and reconstruct a religious tradition with its own tools, including interpretation of dogma and scripture" (2016, 318).

In addition, choosing to be a feminist theologian itself is a claim to agency, which the scholars of GWFS need to recognize when they work with "the lives and thoughts of 'ordinary women' or lay women" (Vuola 2016, 322). The GWFS scholars' focus on everyday life and ordinary believers, Vuola reminds, is a result of the turn toward lived religion where women can claim "some religious authority." Lived religion offers a sphere which is "central for feminist theologians;" however, she warns that without deeper engagement with feminist theology, scholarship on religion and gender may, ironically, reproduce old binaries (323).

At the core of the strong argument that Vuola builds for the GWFS scholars lies a genuine call for "deeper interdisciplinarity" by which she means a "scholarly interest in ideas as much as in practice" (324). This call, I know from experience, requires a massive amount of time and research for whoever self-identifies as a feminist scholar of religion and runs the risk of severe criticism or indifference by theologians regardless of their gender. I actually felt the necessity of obtaining a graduate degree in Theology to underpin my research on lived religion.

I agree with Vuola's reasoning behind why feminist scholars of religion need to be knowledgeable of theology (326-27). However, I have observed that feminist theologians seldom use ethnographic methods or include the anthropologists' insights into religion in developing a feminist theology as Vuola points out. Theologians, including feminist ones, generally employ "textual methods for the interpretation of texts and traditions" thus creating "a vacuum at the heart of feminist theology" (326). One can find a little from women's interpretations of their religious traditions, their ways of acting as religious individuals. In other words, the blind spots go both ways; first, a blindness to theology in anthropology and religious studies; second, a blindness toward different forms of women's everyday practices and their ethnographic study in feminist theology (326). Vuola remains optimistic, particularly in her confidence regarding GWFS, which she claims will "form a privileged space for creating bridges between" the divisions that dragged from the past to the present in the disciplines of religious studies, anthropology, and theology (329).

Lived religion cross-paths with feminist and engaged scholarship in the following ways: History of practical theology includes feminist theology that adopts critical stances and looks for possible contributions from the hermeneutical and the personal. An early attention to this convergence was drawn by Liz Stanley that feminist researchers should transcend the theory/research divide and recognize the symbiotic relationship between manual and intellectual activities (1990, 15). Secondly, a practical theologian is by necessity an engaged scholar and has much in common with the engaged scholars from other disciplines (Ganzevoort and Roeland 2014, 93). Moreover, I have conducted work with underprivileged women and refugees in the areas of peace, justice, and conflict resolution in the past through the lenses of a feminist and an engaged scholar (Ezer 2015, 2017, 2019a, 2020). In retrospect, I recognize that the expressions of lived religion have been present in them but were either unidentified or implicitly touched upon that

I plan to explore in near future. This book aims to be the first major undertaking.

Religion, Spirituality, Lived Religion or Religion-as-Lived

Although I advocate for forging two terms into one (religio-spirituality)[3] and demonstrate substantial evidence of the reasons for this combination and blurred boundaries, I acknowledge the long existing literature that separates religion from spirituality. Religio-spiritual or its noun form (religio-spirituality) contests the notion that treats them as analytically distinct concepts.

The challenges to the distinction between religion and spirituality have been on the rise not only in European and North American context but also across cultures, a phenomenon which is backed up by the results of this study as well. The "practice of intellectually creating in-between spaces has allowed academics" across disciplines to better understand the limitations of the binaries and question their utilities (Day et al. 2013, 2). I choose to allocate a considerable space for the literature that convincingly argues for discarding the dichotomy.

The general assumption is that spirituality is considered more on the individual experience spectrum and does not necessarily operate in an institutional setting. Appropriating a medieval definition, Soelle defines spirituality as "knowledge of God through and from experience," underlining the extraordinariness and non-institutionability of spirituality (2001, 45). That religion mostly refers to human practices and behaviors concerned with seeking the sacred but also often with dogmas, traditions, and institutional regulations, and spirituality, by contrast, is a "continuous quest for the sacred" (Pargament 2007, 32).

Etymologically the English word religion derives from the Latin word *religio*, the idea of a "binding" together and contains the sense of an organized culture that echoes Durkheim's (1976) understanding of religion as a "unified system of beliefs and practices relative to sacred things." By contrast, Smith (1978) critiqued the usefulness of the idea of a religion. Instead, he argued that what described religions are, in fact, historical constructions superimposed upon the diverse experiences of people of personal faith who live within what he calls "cumulative traditions."

A provocative option is offered by Robert Orsi, who retains the word religion but qualifies it as "good" or "true" religion. He tells the readers to

---

[3] I use the term religio-spiritual to forge "spirituality" and "religion" and thus challenge the notion that treat them as analytically distinct concepts.

transpose "true religion" to "spirituality" if they wish, on the understanding that "spirituality" is a term crafted in the U.S. culture to designate the opposite of "bad religion." He calls spirituality "a disciplinary word, built out of and for exclusion" (Orsi 2005, 188). Stephen Taysom, in defense of Orsi's "abundant events" against the ones who criticize him for insulating religion from criticism, finds "Orsi's category potentially appealing" since "Orsi is attempting to create categories that bring religious experience into the 'real' world rather than attempting to fence them off" (2012, 5).

James Murphy argues that popular and academic divisions between religion and spirituality are unfounded. A wider perspective that considers the interplay of many different cultural and social factors on both beliefs and practices is more useful. In the context of a psychological research into religion, his argument supports the basis of this book that working beyond the religion-spirituality distinction offers a "potential to better understand the complexity and diversity of lived religion" (2017, 1).

There is also the concept of "ambiguous sacred between religion and spirituality" which becomes significant in the accounts of the agnostic-atheist Syrian women (Sara, Emilia, and Ola) in relation to spirituality and transcendence (Blasi et al. 2018). They revisit works of Otto (1936) to tackle "the contemporary religion-spirituality divide" to distinguish regular religious practices from mystical experiences. Although Simmel's ideas on inner-life attitudes towards the sacred, and the realm of new practices, vocabulary, and meanings that religiosity-spirituality creates (87) are pregnant for intriguing debates, I only mention them here to remind the reader that there is a whole literature about the sacred-secular divide and in-between spaces (Day et al. 2013; Blasi et al. 2018).

The related sections where the words of the displaced women from Syria take the foreground will demonstrate these above statements further in the book. For the self-proclaimed agnostic-atheists, Sara and Emilia[4], spirituality relates to inexplicable feelings or transcendence (Ezer 2019a, 144-45, 89) yet their descriptions are not too far from the strong believer Zizinia (103-104). Ola, another atheist, is confident of the truthfulness of some "abundant events" (Orsi 2007) that befell on her, and shares them in her interview, naming witnesses to convince me.

There are comprehensive definitions of religion and contemporary discussions on pragmatics of (re)defining religion (Harrison 2006; Koss-Chioino and Hefner 2006; Yandell 1999). Because they occasionally complicate "religion versus spirituality" dichotomy further, I remain in favor

---

[4] Atheist and agnostic are used interchangeably by Emilia and Sara.

of Ruard Ganzevoort's more inclusive definition of religion: "transcending patterns of action and meaning, emerging from and contributing to the relation with the sacred" (2009, n/a). His description acknowledges many practices that fall outside of formal religion. There are also scholars who argue against a separation of religion from spiritualism, particularly in the context of individual transformation and healing (Hogue 2006). Nevertheless, the present day uses of the term spirituality have become so pervasive that incorporating "spirituality" into the concept of "lived religion" (Streib 2008, 54) as a critical proposal prove to be more efficient and supportive of my interview findings. One should also note that "vernacular religion" and "everyday religion" have also gained ground as interchangeable terms in contemporary religious scholarship along with "lived religion."

Another reason for considering Streib's proposal vital is my criticism of the dichotomy between religion and spirituality. His thesis that spirituality can be explained within the framework of religion not only clears the cacophony around multiplying definitions of religion and spirituality but also challenges the limitations of the "religion versus spirituality" binary approach that I have been critical of. A supportive argument, provided by Meredith McGuire, is that "spirituality is closely linked with material human bodies" and the lived religion includes "the myriad individual ways people put [their] stories into practice" (2008, 97-98).

Ammerman's impressive perseverance on mapping out the messy area regarding religion and spirituality is evidenced in her multiple publications. She gathered data derived from individuals' stories to categorize as theistic, extra-theistic, and ethical spiritualities, acknowledging the complexities. Her conclusions (2014b; 2013) invite readers to avoid easy assertions about the absence of religion in a modern world, instead to recognize the overlaps between religion and spirituality. She takes people's practices into account where religious belonging, belief, spirituality and traditions are all implicated in each other. As a sociologist, her criticism is valuable for this book: "Sociologists seeking to understand religion unnecessarily limit the scope of our inquiry, then, when we insist that religion be contained in an authoritative, supernatural realm that is itself contained in recognized institutional boxes [...] Recognizing a wider range of variation will allow us more powerful explanatory models" (2014b, 293).

Ammerman's definition of lived religion ("the embodied and enacted forms of spirituality that occur in everyday life") bridges spirituality and religion (2014a, 189) while Orsi proposes novel concepts such as "abundant events" under the notion of lived religion (2007, 42). I contend that the permeable boundaries of sacred and secular through lived religion need to be taken into account by RFMS scholars too since "the religion people live everyday weaves in and out of the language and symbols and interactions of public spaces and bureaucratized institutions" as much as in the intimacy of homes (Ammerman 2014a, 196).

Another criticism of the religion-spirituality divide comes from eco-theologians and feminists who have argued that such a split is gendered. The division prioritizes the masculine spirit over the feminine material, and devalues the feminined natural world over male-dominated institutions (Day et al. 2013). Those involved in alternative spiritualities often claim that this divide is "not typical of all religions, only certain ones" such as Christianity, and theirs have "no such either/or compartmentalization of the world" (Harvey 1997; Berger et al. 2003). Ager and Ager confirms it in their work on local faith communities: "The Western construct of religion (…) involves the imposition of a spiritual/physical dualism that is inconsistent with the epistemologies of many religious traditions" (2016, 40). Without sweeping assumptions, I think the reader would join me in observing that some of the Syrian women respondents, particularly Zizinia and Dima, grew up in environments with no compartmentalization of spiritualities and religions.

Heather Eaton warned early on against the spirituality versus religion dualism also in the context of ecofeminism. This split, Eaton argued, may cause a neglect in deeply complex histories of existing religious traditions, self-declared spirituals downplaying hegemonic religions as inadequate and/or fundamentalist (1996, 113). As a feminist researcher, I join her argument that the persistence on "divorcing spirituality from religion leaves ecofeminist spiritualities vulnerable to feebleness or fundamentalism," depriving them of "a critical understanding of the relationship between religion and spirituality." Vulnerability she mentions is discernable not only in ecofeminist spiritualities but also in the spiritualities of the women on the move. In fact, I contend that it is via appropriation of the lived religion approach that one can explore further complexities of religions and mend the neglect that Eaton draws attention to. This approach can be used in inquiries into histories of existing traditions, their present states, and projections into their future.

A recent example of the rejection or complication of the "spiritual but not religious" approach is Paola Cavaliere's study (2019). She argues that the religion-spirituality distinction fails to capture the empirical reality of contemporary Japanese religions, and it does not take into account new modalities of experiences of people with religious and spiritual affiliations. Although many spiritual techniques and therapies are foreign imports, their appeal in contemporary societies (whether in the West or the East, such as Turkey, Japan or Syria) should also be considered within the context of the host country's traditions and rituals. Because the host country's heritage already possesses a long history and has been re-interpreted by individualized affiliations. Majority of the Syrian women respondents, particularly the young ones, exemplified the complexity in their accounts, which this study presents as practices of lived religion.

Shakman Hurd argues that lived religion is the religion of much of the world, where it is often difficult to classify individuals as believers or nonbelievers in a single and stable religious (or spiritual, I would add) tradition. While studying religion in three categories, that is, expert religion, lived religion, and governed religion, Hurd defines lived religion as "a diverse field of human activity, relations, investments, beliefs, and practices that may or may not be captured in the set of human goings-on that are identified as 'religion' for the purposes of law and governance" (2015, 8). Following Ammerman's steps, she too acknowledges the blurred boundaries and complex power relations among the three.

Trinka's definition of migrant religion remains among the most incorporating ones for the aim of this book. He understands religion "as a dynamic set of practices, beliefs, and values that, regarding migratory decision-making and travel, includes ritual or petitionary behaviors enacted to access and marshal superhuman entities as well as engagements with religious professionals or humans," (...) for the purposes that include "acquiring supernatural indications or affirmations of human action, obtaining safety or health benefits, engaging religiously-affiliated social networks and sacred spaces" (2019b, 68; 2021, 69). Religion regulates emotions and provides psycho-social support by frameworks that "express and interpret the spectrum of experiences encountered along the way" (2019a, 6).

In summary, the lived religion approach has emerged as a critical academic initiative that can be considered both as a corrective and challenge to more text-based or macro approaches, developing a form of "radical non-reductionism and a preference for ethnographic approaches" (Knibbe 2020, 251). Therefore, many studies that involve fieldwork regarding migrant religion or religion-on-the move present themselves within the framework of lived religion initiatives. Knibbe points to lived religion's directions within the anthropological approaches and links them with feminist thinking on the status and role of academic knowledge.

Lived religion is a new mode of inquiry into religious experience that has started to develop, drawing on phenomenology and on the anthropology of the everyday. Instead of relying on statistical evidence, the lived religion approach investigates religious belief and practice at the micro-level of everyday life (Lynch 2012, 81). It also opens up space for research that engages in selectivies within a religion or across religious traditions, forming a "DIY-kind of religiosity" that is compatible with the rising religious pluralism which is "brought about by globalisation and migration processes" (Anczyk and Grzymała-Moszczyńska 2020, 25-26).

Refugee, Irregular Migrant, Newcomer, or Displaced: Consciously or Politically Defined?

A brief discussion on the terms refugee, migrant, and the category of "women refugees" is apt here. The current use of "refugee" has its roots in the official definition of the 1951 Convention ratified by 145 state parties, and with the establishment of UNHCR. Although the legal definition is available on the United Nations' website, many people (myself included) attempt adopting less stigmatized ("newcomer") or more explanatory terms ("forcibly displaced individual") while acknowledging the occasional necessity in using "refugee" depending on the context. The word refugee refers to a specific legal status whereas "newcomer" does not refer to any type of legal status. However, it can refer to both status holders and asylum seekers; the ones who recently arrived (Gore et al. 2019). I think that the duration of *recently* needs to be specified as in Derks and Srdjan's recent study on Eritrean newcomers in Amsterdam and how they negotiated religion in their process of integration (2020).

Jung and Horstmann aim to validate "refugee-migrant" since they argue that the term considers "the subjective and the legal aspects in the refugee-subject making" and its use "allows for more complexity" (2015, 3). "Irregular migrant" is another term defined by the International Organization of Migration as a "movement that takes place outside the regulatory norms of the sending, transit and receiving country" (IOM, 2011). Other scholars have refined the concepts by dividing the category "migrant" into subcategories, such as migrants from former colonies, privileged migrants, labor migrants, undocumented migrants, asylum seekers and refugees, and the like (Castles and Miller 2009, 4).

The Pew Forum defines an international migrant as someone who has been living for one year or longer in a country other than the one in which he or she was born. This means that many foreign workers and international students are counted as migrants. Additionally, the U.N. considers refugees and, in some cases, their descendants such as Palestinians born in refugee camps to be international migrants. Van der Veer reminds that legally the distinction between migrant and refugee is pertinent, but the boundaries between these two categories are dynamic and arbitrary. Asylum is a protection of a foreigner under threat and what is being assessed in juridical procedures in the receiving country is the legibility and accuracy of this threat (2021, 3).

Trinka's significant work on migration and religion (2019a, 2019b; 2021) remains in the fields of lived religion and refugee studies although he consistently prefers to use migrant over refugee with the "assumption that all refugees are migrants, but not all migrants are refugees." In doing so, he often uses migrant as the broader category and poses a justified criticism against an overemphasis on reading scriptural narratives as "refugee literature." I join his tending to the ways in which scholars can speak "with greater nuance about various experiences of religión on-the-move" and present this book also within a larger pattern or patterns of "religion on-the-move" (personal communication, February 16, 2021).

However, I acknowledge the fact that there has been no consensus on these categories, and the distinctions among these terms still remain rather fluid. Further debates and coinages are likely to emerge, pointing at the intricacies of the individuals in transition as the term refugee continues to stigmatize certain people on media (Andrejč 2018; Becker 2018; Frederiks 2016).

CHAPTER III

REPRESENTATIONS AND AGENCY

This chapter presents a review of academic work on representations of Muslim refugees, women refugees, and Muslim women refugees in the Global North with a focus on Europe and the concept of agency. A few complementary studies are mentioned that are conducted in Turkey and Lebanon, and some studies didn't specify the religious background of the subjects but only the country of forced departure. The rapid increase in the number of critical studies regarding representations and stereotypes of newcomers presents a promising picture in raising awareness on the issue (Kokkonen 2017; Dückelmann 2018; Yalouri 2019; Anderson 2020; Aswad 2020, Bye 2020; Horvat 2020; Walczak and Lampas 2020; Negura, Buhay, and de Rosa 2021). However, most scholars continue to feed into the terminology by repeated use of the problematic terms such as refugee and "refugee crisis." Moreover, there is a striking erasure of gender in these texts which is concerning from a feminist viewpoint.

In her criticism of refugee representations, Kate Smith points to how "public perceptions of refugees are primarily represented as male, overlooking women's stories and allowing for men's stories to be dominant narratives told about refugee's lives" (2015, 462). She argues that direct narratives of women refugees serve to disrupt dominant narratives and support producing a counter narrative, to which this book also contributes. Smith concludes that it is time to look into "the forms of assemblages" for "more nuanced understandings of displaced women's agency against the dehistoricized representations of victimized refugee women" (2018, 57).

The Syrian women's accounts in this book contribute to the growing body of ethnographic data which indicates that migrants "draw on, adapt, and add to their religious toolkits throughout their moves in order to accomplish physical, social, and spiritual ends" (Trinka 2019, 4). They challenge and transform the passive, silent, and repressed women stereotypes in the constructed images mostly shaped by the media in the Global North. Trinka also highlights a recent "methodological turn-to-the-migrant" effect on the agency of the displaced, which simultaneously affects the representations of the people-on-the-move. Models in economics and politics, that is, the focus on risk-reward or cost-benefit, were recognized as the dominant reasons for human migration. These models, however, generally have failed to account for "the migrant as an active agent in a matrix of other sociocultural contingencies" (2019, 3).

Ghorashi's regular focus on migrant and refugee women's agency over 15 years contributed significantly to the engaged academia. Probably her own history as once an Iranian refugee now naturalized Dutch citizen has a role in her dedication to the improvement of integration policies of the Netherlands. In one of her latest articles (2021), she revisits two earlier research, demonstrating how dialogical narratives helped "refugee women find their voices, their passions and thus their agency, which was forgotten or marginalised." This negligence and marginalization were because of the normalizing power of the dominant discourses that erased refugee women's agency by portraying them as "weak, lacking quality and being non-emancipated" (59). The disruption of normalized images and actions via "narrative engaged research" such as women-only life writing groups created a "partial and temporal possibility to break away from the dominant fixed image of refugee women as people with shortcomings, which in turn created a potential for acting differently" (59). That sharing narratives of the past can help finding unlikely commonalities while bringing agency to the participants resonates with my choice for interviewing over other methods.

Ayhan Kaya criticizes Refugee Studies in Turkey for its lack of anthropological research which permits "the refugees to speak for themselves," thus recognizing the missing element of agency of the displaced individuals in the Turkish context (2017, 368). His work on Istanbul as a city of Syrian refugees is significant but fails indicating a gender-specification, a much needed component in RFMS. My focus is on the agency of women as actors on the move who can re-negotiate and re-create authoritative ways of performing and interpreting religious or faith-centered traditions.

Encountering a whole section (Part II: Deconstructing the Muslim Refugee) in the edited collections such as *The Refugee Crisis and Religion* (Mavelli and Wilson 2017) is a promising development with 4 out of 16 chapters displaying studies that challenge the public imaginary or the negative representations of refugees with a focus on their religion. A preconceived fear of judgment by the members of the host community affects the self-image of the newcomers and causes stress and discontent at times (Harandi 2019; Beaman, Selby, and Barras 2017). Although refugees have to deal with more pressing non-religious concerns in their new environment, the questions around presumed religious identity can be very annoying, even leading to giving up socialization. I argue that language use in all aspects of daily and academic life is extremely significant in order to achieve true and long-term inclusion of the displaced individuals.

In a book that underlines the concepts of relationality and agency throughout, referring to some recent studies positively where a problematic jargon or language use in a certain circle (e.g., social work) is endorsed may seem conflicting. A perfect example is the study below published in an international journal of public health in its analysis of social representations of Canadian caseworkers who have been working with refugees. Canada welcomed 46,700 refugees on humanitarian grounds in 2016 alone, setting a new record since the immigration act was adopted in 1978 and more than 25,000 refugees were Syrians. As a result, helping professionals feel overloaded and poorly equipped to adequately address the needs of refugees (Negura, Buhay, and de Rosa 2021).

Regarding the workers' perception and understanding of the otherness in the refugee or "the new Canadian" and the self (caseworker) encounters, the study concludes very positively. However, unlike the studies that I have referred to so far in the literature review on representations, the authors introduce a different definition, that is, social representation and explain its use. They define it as "a theory of common sense about an object of significance to a social group" that is produced by logic and social thought, orienting individuals in their environments. It is supposed to enable communication in a community through a shared code for social exchange, naming, and other aspects of the social world (2021, 2).

Social representations are created and transformed through two processes that the authors name as "anchoring and objectification." Through objectification, an abstract concept such as refugee becomes "concrete and operational" and through anchoring, this object becomes familiar via "the insertion of the object within a known system of reference, such as lived experience that facilitates the mastering of the representational object, namely, refugees" (2). Do I share the gestures of shaking my head and/or rolling my eyes with the readers of this book as a response to the quotation? The authors' reference to "lived experience" is not enough to endorse the jargon use although reading the selected firsthand accounts of the participants (15 caseworkers in total) was uplifting. Besides, the participants' words serve positively for my study as they exclusively constructed representations of Syrian refugees based on their experiences by using the words resilient, strong, and competent. Some of them included their own experiences as migrants in the past.

It wouldn't be misleading to derive from their conclusion and the analysis of the data that the three authors' aim was to reveal and distribute knowledge that would benefit refugees' wellbeing and to contribute to the positive representations of the newcomers. However, statements that include word choices such as "the mastering of the representational object, namely, refugees" (Negura, Buhay, and de Rosa 2021, 2) are evidence to the discipline-specific academic jargon that some researchers who work at independent and liminal spaces like myself have trouble with. The three authors' affiliations (School of Social Work, University of Ottawa and Department of Social and Developmental Psychology, Sapienza University of Rome) confirm my initial concerns expressed in the Introduction about the lack of or miscommunication across disciplines. A theologian or Religious Studies scholar would be using different terms.

Nevertheless, the article reveals promising language use as well, especially when the overworked caseworkers simultaneously perceive Syrian refugees as "strong and suffering" and "vulnerable but also resilient" (8-9) which the authors call "a dual representation" (9). They keenly distinguish it from the cliché and dangerous binaries of "victims vs invaders" or "useful resource vs threat" that are mostly provocatively (invaders, threat) or naively (victims, useful resources) produced by the media and/or fundraising agencies. The dual representations are "empathy-informed" recognitions in the same displaced individual regarding resilience and capacity of adaptation along with the vulnerability. That is why I include this study as an example to academic studies that are demonstrative of positive and novel approaches to refugee representations in Social Sciences while appropriating an old and problematic terminology.

Debates on Depicting Women Refugees/Newcomers

Constructing representations of female refugees has always been a contested subject due to the humanitarian discourses' use of images "to broadcast a narrative about rescue and compassion" (Fadlalla 2009, 79) "to attract funding" with an "emphasis on vulnerability" of women rather than forming a politicized language "around entitlement and claiming rights" (Kiwan 2016, 157). Kiwan rightly points to the tensions within the policy discourse of UNHCR and argues for a bolder, more holistic, and contextualized approach. This involves recognizing the refugee as a whole person who moved from one particular socio-political context into a new one (160). Her article is valuable in its introduction of Syrian women refugees' initiatives across countries to prove agency (161-165).

Before proceeding with other scholars' work on the topic, let me share a personal anecdote as evidence of how insidiously and unlikely a stereotype can be reproduced. After five years of hard work, I submitted my book on Syrian women to my publisher in North Carolina whose editorial team was close to perfect; always responsive, punctual, and respectful of my choices as a writer during the process. Thus, you can imagine my shock when the initial cover photo of the book (Ezer 2019a) was forwarded to me for confirmation: The face of a young, full lipped brunette with a black headscarf, large dark eyes, and smooth skin. I was speechless for some hours before gathering myself and writing an email to the chief editor about the striking contrast between the cover photo and the content of the book. The editors apologized and asked me to take over the issue. I approached an Amsterdam-based young female Syrian artist, Yara Said, who responded immediately after checking the cover photo which was already online for pre-order promotion. We decided to illustrate a real photo with a background set in nature as most Syrian women often recalled the mountains that they went for picnics or camping. Said created a highly praised cover illustration that satisfied all of us, inspired by one of the photos sent by Muzna Dureid who features in the book. The urgent corrective was made collaboratively, and the case was closed.

The outcome of the promoted visuals of women does not always have this happy end, the corrective intervention which was received without an objection. For example, Aswad's recent analysis of refugee representations of the International Rescue Committee (IRC) is disheartening but pointing to an imperialist epistemology. Her findings suggest that despite positive overtures, the IRC's refugee discourse is consistent with hegemonic media discourses of the racialized Other. Without denying the narrative's potency, Aswad questions the rhetorical construction of Syrian refugees through existing power structures in which the refugee's "agentic voice becomes a mouthpiece for American exceptionalist rhetoric and quixotic narratives delineating America as a utopian benefactor" of humankind (2020, 40-41). "The refugee is stripped of biographical specificity" and construed only through existence within the nation's borders (34). Ironically, Aswad's analysis lacks intersectionality and that the phrase "Syrian refugee" is used too generically, reproducing the issues that she problematizes in her analysis of the IRC's videos.

Yumna Asaf's article "Syrian Women and the Refugee Crisis" is another reminder that the narrative of war in general "fetches the image of women as victims only" which "takes away their agency and leaves them unheard in the rebuilding of their country" (2017, 14). Even if they are survivors of a conflict with patterns of violence, it does not exclude or prevent women from active participation in peace building efforts. In other words, Asaf draws attention to the possibility of two simultaneous images regarding refugee women: the victim of conflict, the hero of peace negotiations, that is, if one cannot or does not want to drop the survivor's vulnerability.

That some Syrian women explicitly refuse to be positioned as migrants or refugees is therefore not surprising. Their resistance stems from "the widespread negative stereotypical image of refugees" in the dominant narrative of the Syrian War, that is, they are "poor, needy and helpless people, worthy of charity" (Shalaby 2018, 473). Kumsa's empirical study in Toronto despairingly shows that the refugee is constructed "as a strong antithesis of the nation," resulting in the several problematic dichotomies (nation has state; refugee is stateless; nation has country; refugee is placeless, and so forth). Thus the young women whom Kumsa interviewed distance themselves from the refugee position, that is, "the displaced person with no country, the dangerous roamer and unattached wanderer outside the family of nations" (2006, 244).

My hesitation to include Abu-Lughod's decades-long work on Muslim women in this section stems from doing injustice to her oeuvre and also because locating her work into multiple subsections of this book is possible. Abu-Lughod has struggled to reconcile the problematic images of women victimized by Islam with the complex Muslim women she has known through her research in various communities. That she used the almost same title for her book in 2013 which she used for her groundbreaking article "Do Muslim Women Really Need Saving?" (2002) is disconcerting for me. Her persistence in revealing conditions of gender inequalities from a wider web, that is, the global interconnections that implicate the Global North is a major contribution to representation analysis of Muslim women. That Abu-Lughod presents vignettes of the lives of ordinary women who practice Islam to tackle the standard Western vocabulary of oppression, choice, and agency serves to the current debates in lived Islam from my view.

Shalaby underlines the deployment of agency by the Syrian women whom she interviewed through some discourse strategies and performance devices in their narratives (2018, 473-76). They disassociate themselves from refugee category on the basis of three characteristics, "what they have, what they do and where they stand," identified by van Dijk (1998, 154) as I too made the effort to point out these three in the individuals' life stories in my previous work (Ezer, 2019a). More specifically, their agency was constructed with an emphasis on education, finances, and work; that is; they all were active even under the circumstances, and not idle or parasitic beings in the dynamics of their new country's system.

In "Can the Irregular Migrant Woman Speak?" Synnøve Bendixsen (2016) responds to the fluctuating representations of Ethiopian female irregular migrants in Norway. She argues that there is space for migrant women's voice and political action which are shaped by representations of gender, subject positions, and socio-cultural perceptions, but somehow women need to perform in culturally and socially acceptable ways. The discourse around their political actions exemplifies how public spheres remain to be shaped by class, race, gender, and ethnicity regardless of legal status. Some of the Ethiopians in her study were Muslims but their religious identity "was silenced during the [women's] demonstrations" (244).

Sara Silvestri is among the major critics of the Muslim women images in Europe (2011; 2012). Not understood as agents of their own lives, she accurately argues, they are "perceived as passive dependent variables of far-away political and geographical contexts." That their universes are often "reduced to attributed identities and superficial debates around their clothes" renders them as victims of patriarchal cultures and of an "oppressive backward religion" and "of the racism and prejudices of European societies." Silvestri's frustration by the public discussions that "focus on one-sided portrayals of the Muslim women who inhabit Europe" rather than citizens (2011, 1233) is in line with the contributors of Moghissi and Ghorashi's edited work *Muslim Diaspora in the West* (2010).

Exploring the intersections between lived experiences, everyday concerns, and conceptualizations of faith beyond the traditional religion among women in five countries from a gender perspective, Silvestri presents a timely and significant corrective to the relevant literature. Her criticism of so called "Muslim Diaspora" also responds to a similar issue (though not gender specific) where Silvestri analyzes this sweeping term to challenge the injustice done to the pluralism and disagreements that exist within Islam (2016). Reinhart's more recent study shares her criticism with its claim that "the diaspora of Islam is much larger than the set of actual travelers," especially due to the technological tools that enable constant virtual travels and presences (2020, 157).

In a slightly different context, Marjo Buitelaar's interviews with Moroccan migrants' daughters reveal the women's concerns on popular negative representations of Islam in the Netherlands, something they do not wish to feed via narrations. Buitelaar challenges the second generation Muslim women's images via the rearticulations of Hajj/pilgrimage storytelling and provides agency to them. Her critical analysis includes further complications such as the women's frustration of having to prove that they are "good" Muslims. Whatever they say, they remain concerned with negative portrayals so most tend not to cooperate in research. Consequently, Muslims who are already motivated to discuss commonalities and/or differences between Muslim and non-Muslim European citizens are overrepresented in interview projects such as the one on which her article is based (2020, 15).

Another example to such projects is by Österlind and Minganti who demonstrate an alleged "demand from both Muslim and non-Muslim audiences for young women to act as public representatives of a distinctly modern and Swedish Muslim identity" (2016, 42). Österlind and Minganti argue that this is part of an ongoing generational shift away from the first-generation immigrant men and women converts, who occupied the front figure positions for Muslims in Sweden. They also claim that many young Muslim women decide to step into the realm of public struggle to be recognized as full subjects and citizens which requires visibility, particularly through media appearances (41). Their attempts ironically lead to silencing other Muslim women, about which Buitelaar cautioned since they steer to misleading knowledge production via overrepresentation.

One affirmative answer to an above mentioned article, "Can the Irregular Migrant Woman Speak?" comes from Muzna Dureid. Taken from a paper she wrote for one of her graduate courses at Concordia University in Canada, the following passage impeccably captures the issue of refugee representations and its impact on refugees in the words of a newcomer:

> Refugees are always being judged by their failures. If they cannot succeed in crossing the ocean, escaping the borderline, passing an exam, finding a job, or making money, they apparently do not deserve the opportunity that has been gifted to them. They must be both heroes and victims but never normal human beings. And yet, despite this stigma, there is always a Refugees Welcome sign wherever they go and this can be very confusing. (Ezer 2019a, 64)

Muzna's repeated desire to be "normal" is not unique to this passage and is used liberally in her interviews so it calls for a definition. From the context, it can be gathered that letting go of a stigma is part of this normalcy but I ask for further clarification. Muzna doesn't hesitate: "Normal is being free from guilt and fear. I don't want to feel guilty for where I am today but I cannot help it" (64).

Birgit Meyer's drawing attention to a collective amnesia in Europe explicates Muzna's language use further. Meyer problematizes the crisis framing in "the sense of exceptionality and extraordinariness" that accompanies the term crisis (2021, 260). If people can overcome this historical amnesia, in the framework of the so-called refugee crisis, a basic insight presents itself: The 2015 moment of large groups of refugees into Germany is merely a moment in a long history of forced, partly forced, and relatively unforced movement of people in Europe and the rest of the world and thus it is "not an exceptional crisis" (Gatrell 2019, 187). Normalizing people's movements across regions will eventually affect the representations of the people-on-the-move, and result in less stigmatized refugee depictions in Europe.

Lena Gemzöe, Marja-Liisa Keinänen, and Avril Maddrell draw attention to the "almost obsessive focus on the Muslim woman in political and scholarly debate" while problematizing the lack of analytical attention to the intersection of religion and gender in migration processes, and the significance of religion to immigrant populations in Europe (2016, 20). They acknowledge the shift in feminist theory in which religion is being readdressed but they rightly question that it is the more "visible and identifiable veiled Muslim women" who have attracted huge scholarly attention, not the Christian women in Europe (6). There are, however, many invisible, that is, unveiled Muslim women in the Global North whose faith practices (and many other concerns) remain unstudied in the field of religion and gender. My book also helps fill this gap.

"Can the Displaced Speak?" is an ethnographic study conducted in a high school in Western Canada with Muslim refugee girls who negotiate their identity and belonging through photovoice method. Miled is exceptionally careful in her language (referring to the students as co-researchers) and methodology since at the time of the study most of the girls were not comfortable in English yet. Photovoice method, Miled convincingly demonstrates, creates new media forms that challenge the homogenizing, colonial and orientalist representations around Muslim women and refugees (2020). Adopting the feminist praxis-oriented approach, inspired by an earlier study in Canada (Sutherland and Cheng 2009), Miled's efforts stand out to empower the Muslim refugee girls and have concrete results. Three exhibitions took place at the school, the university, and at a local church, each attracting a different audience.

Finally, a corrective acknowledgement is needed not only about the image of the Muslim women but also about the representation of the religious women in general as Gemzöe, Keinänen, and Maddrell mention in *Contemporary Encounters* (2016, 7). Referencing to a pioneering study by Mahmood (2006) within the postcolonial feminist theory, that the image of the religious woman is no longer a "passive receiver of patriarchal ideology," they warn readers against any theoretical oversimplification and perpetuation of inherent power relations between the Global North and South (2016, 9). Gemzöe, Keinänen, and Maddrell accurately argue that feminist interventions in the academia "must reject" attempts of measuring "other cultures" -or religions for that matter- in relation to the supposedly superior women representations in "Euro-American culture in the feminist analytical frame" (9). Implicit judgements can be embedded in many of us as scholars and might lead to losing sight of the similarities between gendered power dynamics across religious and cultural boundaries.

Religio-Spirituality, Resilience, and Post Traumatic Growth (PTG)

Integration of religio-spirituality into lived religion (or religion-as-lived) terminology will enrich the discussion on refugees' experiences about displacement and religion. However, the complexity of the topic becomes even more entangled due to the specific regional and familial faith-based practices, and their impact on refugee psyche. Particularly, in regard to religion's links to coping and resilience, I agree with Kenneth Pargament's statement that these connections cannot be comprehended "through the person, the situation, or the context alone." It is "the interplay of these forces" which determines the ebb and flow of religion and coping on the shores of intricacies (1997, 162). McGuire welcomes these combined forces by putting "spirituality" in brackets and defining it as "the everyday ways ordinary people attend to their spiritual lives" (2008, 98).

Cornelis Laban's reference to religion remains positive in connection to resilience and is free of inverted commas of McGuire's spirituality. As an "organized form of spirituality," Laban argues that religion can be considered an interpretation frame (2015, 202). It can strengthen one's perseverance to live while providing a feeling to be part of a larger union, an emotional and social support of communities. In short, he concludes that religion can be an important source of resilience; thus, should be paid attention to continuously (203).

I define resilience as a positive behavioral adaptation after encountering adversity or trauma while post traumatic growth (PTG) refers to the positive psychological changes that individuals report after difficult life circumstances. These changes encompass personal relationships, new plans about the future, increasing personal strength, self-reliance, and appreciation for life as well as spiritual changes. Deliberate rumination (a subsequent process of reflection and purposeful re-examination of the trauma) and social support have been important factors in explaining PTG rather than persistent negative syndromes (Tedeschi and Calhoun 1995; Tedeschi et al. 2017), which can be observed in the Syrian women's accounts regardless of their faith commitments or practices.

In her work on Syrian religious minorities in Jordan, Khatereh Egdamian (2017) argues that religion creates a sense of solidarity and cohesiveness between refugees (Syrians and Iraqis) who experience exclusion and isolation in their settlements. It also helps them to cope with hardship and adversities and to transcend discriminations of populations in host countries. Similarly, Roger B. Alfani contends in a different context (Africa) that religion "plays an important role in the construct of refugees' resilience" (2021, 89). Eric Trinka recognizes religion as a "source of emotional resilience and of individual and corporate support" and a means by which "movers meet physical and spiritual needs" while negotiating their identity reconfigurations on the move and beyond (2019a, 4). In the context of immigrant mental health in Canada, Chaze et al. review more than two decades of literature to demonstrate the importance of beliefs, religion, and spirituality. They conclude with an urgent call for mental health professionals to take into account their service users' cultural, spiritual, and religious beliefs (2015).

Jacqueline Maria Hagan describes religion as a "powerful guiding, coping, protective, and mediating force," argues that it shapes migrants' decisions to journey, how they decide on the timing of their departures, how they experience the journey, and how they make sense of their place in the migration process. For some, their faith, "expressed in the everyday religious and cultural practices" along the route, did "fortify them with the willpower to persevere" and ultimately reach their destination (2008, 156). Her book stands out in its inclusion of earlier and unexplored stages of the migration process, that is, decision making, the departure, the journey, and the arrival vis-à-vis religion's own transformation, that is, its becoming stronger and more dynamic during the course of the journey. Considered within a larger narrative, she portrays migrants as agents in the transformation of religio-spiritual and cultural practices, as I have attempted here.

One of the Syrian respondents in my study confirms the conclusions above based on her keen observations since the beginning of the war. Dima (31) who grew up as a Sunni Muslim with a secular single mother replied whether she can name something beneficial about Islam in the following words:

> One of the good things I believe is the feeling that power of real religion gives to the people. I mean… I'll give you examples so you know… There are displaced people in Syria and some of them, they've nothing, only God to pray to protect them, and this kind of feeling, it keeps them alive and in power. They have the feeling that they will be protected during hard times. I get that when I speak to the people as an insider because
>
> I'm in contact with them all the time. When they say it, I totally understand it. Like the air strikes, we're running, we're freezing, we don't have anything, no power, no money but at the same time we

have *rahmat* of Allah, which is the mercy of God on us. I think, for the people who believe in God, and take this in their lives, their bad times are gonna be easier for them. That's one thing I like about religion.[5]

Dima is referring to an Islam that serves as a foundation of emotional resilience and individual support, and a means by which the displaced people meet physical and spiritual needs that Trinka mentions above. The mercy of God empowers them to persevere and overcome the challenging times that they are exposed to. When I ask her whether she belongs to this group that she clearly describes, there is a brief silence and hesitation despite the word "insider" that she chose to use for herself: "I went through a lot but … I'm still … you know… I cannot have a category for the realization that I have with God, I still need some time to answer the question."

Kanal and Rottmann's article on refugee women's agency is based on 33 semi-structured interviews with Syrian women in Turkey (2021). Their findings are structured around stressors and coping strategies among which is religious coping. The concepts that emerged repeated among the interviewees were linked to the Islamic values of "patience, thankfulness, gratefulness and satisfaction" with which the women "concretely referenced in" the Quran (8). Resilience was also connected to motherhood and several of the participants mentioned the "importance of teaching gratefulness to" children lead them "to be resilient and agentic" (8).

Religious coping among religious minority refugee women emerged also in a study by Shaw et al. (2019) which draws from feminist theory and intersectionality, presenting women's experiences with religio-spirituality across a wide range of domains. They interviewed 36 forced migrant Shia Muslim women whose first asylum country was predominantly Sunni Muslim. The analysis demonstrates the necessity of support and recognition for the service organizations regarding religious coping among refugee women. Their conclusion endorses the role of religion that Hagan describes above as a "powerful guiding, coping, protective, and mediating force" (2008, 156).

Hagan and Ebaugh (2006) investigate the role of religion in the six stages of the migration process, as they criticize the negligence by both immigration and sociology of religion scholars. Their article draws on the migratory and religious history of a Maya community whose members resettled in the western highlands of Guatemala and Houston, Texas. Their study reveals how migrants use religion in 1) the decision making; 2) preparing for the trip;

---

[5] Selected interview passages by Lubna until here were recorded on 16 February 2020.

3) the journey; 4) the arrival; 5) the role of the ethnic church in immigrant settlement; and 6) the development of transnational linkages, all of which mark the stages of the migration process (2006). In regard to the studies on the intersections of gender and religion in migration processes and the importance of religion to immigrant populations, Lena Gemzöe, Marja-Liisa Keinänen, Avril Maddrell declare that there is still a long way to go (2016, 20).

Anczyk and Grzymala-Moszczynska draw attention to the lack of "cross disciplinary" conversations in religious studies and the field of psychology of religion (2020). Among the three challenges that they identify in intersections of the two is "responses to societal challenges," in which migration processes and religious pluralism are included (26). They propose "participatory action research" (PAR) because of its claims of providing agency to participants and community support (26). Particularly in the European context, Anczyk and Grzymala-Moszczynska contend that PAR may "challenge the EU policies" which attempted to confine religion to a private domain (27).

My study confirms the above mentioned scholars' fieldwork results and their interpretations of them. It also contributes to and juxtaposes the findings with a non-scholars' data, that is, the Syrian women respondents' own words on the topic. Religio-spiritual coping is among the coping strategies that many women-on-the-move utilize while building or reflecting on resilience.

Women's Lived Religion and Feminists' Religio-Spiritualities

The challenges of dismantling or moving beyond dualisms in the knowledge making seem to be persistent also in the literature that is relevant to this section. Among them are "religion as practiced" (lived religion) versus "religion as prescribed" as well as "the religion of the women and private space" versus "the institutionalized public religion" which includes the highbrow theory produced in academia. I remain of the opinion that lived religion and theoretical religion are closely related. A visible negligence in theology in reference to women's religio-spiritualities is problematized by several scholars. Kristen Aune's work (2014) presents a well-established solution by suggesting feminist spirituality as lived religion and is expanded below.

Regarding women's lived religion, McGuire points to the need "to appreciate their ritual practices centered on the so-called private, domestic, familial sphere" because these are the spaces where women's roles - traditionally more passive or non-existent- are "likely to be more active and expressive" (2008, 108). These practices are "at least as important as participation in the public" but visibly neglected in academia (108). Zarkov adds to the argument that "the role of faith in women's everyday life is often ignored, even more often seen as a symbol of traditionalism and backwardness, an obstacle to emancipation" (2015, 6).

One needs to be cautious of the duality between "religion as practiced" (lived religion) and "religion as prescribed" by religious institutions. This is potentially problematic since it might reproduce binary hierarchies between practice and theory, low and high religion, and popular and academic work. As a gender scholar, I am not in favor of an arbitrary separation between those who do/practice religion and those who think and write about it. Although the main data and arguments in this book are meant for being a part of the studies in lived religion and societal changes, I think lived religion and theoretical religion (considered in the realm of theologians) are related. As Helmer reminds us, "theology must engage in religion also on empirical terms and with respect to living relationships," whereas Religious Studies must appreciate the importance of the conceptual and make efforts to "understand the conceptual dimensions in the reality that it studies" (2012, 253). Hers is one of the bridging and dialogical contributions between the two fields.

Likewise, Line Nyhagen contributes to the feminist sociology of religion that favors an open rather than a pre-determined view of what "religion" is and means to women, and it is a plea for a sociology of religion that is empirically grounded in women's lives (2017, 495). She promotes adopting a lived religion approach with an intersectional perspective on religio-spiritual women's identities. In this model, women of any belief can have an active and self-reflexive role in negotiating and changing their own beliefs and practices without discarding institutional attributes of religion that they may engage with. In short, Nyhagen is also against reproducing binary hierarchies, particularly within a feminist framework.

In an edited collection, a contribution to "the so far limited feminist scholarship on religion and intersectionality," Nyhagen and Halsaa define lived religion as "a holistic approach to religion as belief and practice" and underline its "private and individual aspects, as well as public and collective dimensions of everyday religion" (2016, 58, 38). They pose lived religion as a scholarly challenge to "the constructed binary between public and private spheres, as well as the gendering of this distinction" (40).

Kristin Aune's article "Feminist Spirituality as Lived Religion" is significant for this book as it challenges religion-spiritual dichotomy and uses only self-identified feminist women as subjects in a U.K. context. Drawing on Hall, Ammerman, McGuire and Orsi's work, Aune advocates studying feminist spiritualities as examples of lived religion, since they exist beyond religious institutions, and are grounded in everyday practice, emotion and materiality, and often merge aspects from different faiths.

Rather than equating feminism with secularism, secularization, or alternative spiritualities, the article reveals the complex ways of feminists' forging religio-spiritual lives. Religion and spirituality prove to be complex, lived phenomena for these British feminists. Aune identifies three characteristics of feminists' approaches to religion and spirituality: They are de-churched, are relational, and emphasize practice; and these features warrant a new and lived approach to feminists' relationships with religio-spirituality (2014,122). She also refers to the literature that mentions three trajectories in feminists' engagement with religion: feminist secularism and secularization, the feminist turn to spirituality, and religio-spiritual feminist groups (127).

Her research shows that what matters for the feminists she interviewed was practice, leading Aune to conclude that lived religion is the most adequate conceptualization of feminist religio-spiritual approaches. Building on empirical studies of religious feminism, Aune argues for a novel conceptualization of feminist religio-spiritual approaches as lived religion. Her article stands out as an endorsement of the concept of lived religion through the interviewed feminists who "forge religio-spiritual lives in ways that are de-churched, relational, and oriented towards practice" (142). For the WGFS scholars, it demonstrates "the importance of taking seriously the role spirituality and religion play in feminists' lives" and for scholars of religion, "it challenges the conceptual dichotomy between religion and spirituality" (142). My only criticism is her use of "spirituality," "religion," and "religiospiritual" interchangeably throughout the discussion. I would have chosen one of them as I do in this book.

Fedele and Knibbe (2012) also reject the spirituality/religion distinction in their ethnographic work on gender and spirituality. Since there is no clear difference between people who describe themselves as spiritual and those calling themselves religious, many people see themselves as both. Beaman and Beyer (2013), Eccles (2018), and Hurd (2015) are among the scholars who explore suitable methods to research women from a broad range of traditions in their attempts to challenge the previously (often male) defined categories. Eccles in particular underlines the significance of lived realities of women: "our subjects deserve their own, which reflect their lives as they live them, not a standard textbook off-the-shelf model" (2018, 79), a stance that is in close affinity to Aune's.

CHAPTER IV

SCHOLARSHIP ON MUSLIMS, LIVED RELIGION IN ISLAM, AND MUSLIM WOMEN IN EUROPE

Silences, Invisibilities, and Their Discontents: Churchification and Other Research Glitches

A probable reason for the dearth of studies on Muslim refugee women's faith practices relates to the problematics of methods in the study of Muslims in general and to the knowledge production dynamics in Religious Studies. The focus on institutionalized forms of Islam can be attributed to the practical fact that they are easier to locate when researchers plan to carry out fieldwork and interviews. This results in making the non-organized Muslims invisible on an academic level, particularly women. In the case of the interviewed Syrian women refugees, the problem of silencing emerges in triple forms: They are women, refugees, and lacking an active relationship to Islam such as an affiliation with an FBO or mosque. This includes the Syrian women with hijab, which is the most visible sartorial marker for the Muslim woman, but also a misleading one in the Global North.

With the exception of three agnostic-atheist Syrian women, the respondents fall in the middle of the spectrum. They personally and privately identify with Islam in some form or another but do not claim ties to an institutionalized religion. They have built an implicit relationship to Islam, also termed "implicit religion" (Davie 1990). In other words, the interviewed women's common denominator is Islam not only as religion but also as culture, which includes believing without belonging, practicing without affiliation (Spahić Šiljak 2012). The practices and interpretations of Islam disclosed by the interviewed women render this study unique, and suggest further research for a more balanced and realistic data through questioning the methods and contexts in the study of Muslim refugees, particularly of women.

Researchers of contemporary Islam regarding the interpretation of Muslim identity rarely took lived religion into consideration. The gap between "researchers' Islam and Muslims' Islam" is unlikely to be narrowed down in near future; thus, the need to engage in "interpretations of interpretations of Islam" remains (Bectovic 2012, 11). Bectovic also draws on the geographical differences in the scholarship of Religious Studies (to which I add RFMS) and the impact of non-academic and mediatic knowledge of Islam, but especially "the interaction between the humanistic tradition with historical and cultural ways to knowledge of Islam and the tradition of the social sciences." Referring to the work of Stokes and Donnan (2002, 2-4), Bectovic argues that to "have an interdisciplinary approach to Islam requires also an interdisciplinary critique of academic studies" (2012, 22). This statement aptly captures my concerns and criticism of the current literature in RFMS and Religious Studies due to my present academic engagement in both and extends beyond them.

Nadia Fadil's criticism on the predicaments of studying Islam in Europe is also explanatory and sound, and should be extended beyond the continent. The first impasse refers to the historical marking of Islam as Europe's Other; the second interrelated epistemological impasse concerns a "disciplinary nervousness" that she observes among anthropologists' claim makings regarding the Islamic tradition (2019, 121). Getting trapped in a Eurocentric approach may lead to multiple silences and can be a major concern both for the Muslim interlocutors and feminist researchers who are sensitive about giving voice to the other, and not leaving the interlocutors with an uncomfortable feeling (Buitelaar 2020, 15). A similar sensitivity is expressed in the edited collection of *Contemporary Encounters in Gender and Religion* by all its contributors (2016).

Regarding the studies on Islam, Dessing, Jeldtoft, and Woodhead (2013) propose focusing on people's everyday lives by concentrating on how Muslims in Europe live out their faith in workplaces, schools, and home space. Their edited collection also includes how Muslims deal with problems of health, wellbeing, and relationships. It offers empirical data on everyday/lived Islam with its new approach to official religion and tactical religion in relation to one another. Likewise, Shakman Hurd outlines the blurred boundaries and complex power relations among expert religion, lived religion, and governed religion in her book (2015). In an earlier work, Jeldtoft similarly argues that "being a Muslim is not just something that you are, but also that you can actively choose to do" (2012, 31).

Mohaghegh Harandi's MA thesis presents a succinct discussion under the sub-section entitled "Daily life practices and individualization of religion among Muslim immigrants" (2019, 15-16). Her focus remains exclusively on the international Muslim students, similar to Berghammer and Fliegenschnee (2014) whose work is on first-generation female Turkish and Bosnian migrants in Austria, and Bendixsen (2013) who interviewed young Muslim women in Berlin.

Zamila Karimi's "Informal Sacred Spaces of Worship in the Interstices: Lived Religion" (2010) uses lived religion only in its title and discusses the temporarily transformed mundane spaces into sacred environment by practicing certain rituals and customs by the Muslim Diaspora. It demonstrates the diversity among worshippers and their pluralistic customs through analyzing urban spaces such as New York and Montreal. Each study is valuable and unique in its niche focus; however, they all lack female newcomers' voices among the minorities that they produce knowledge about.

A corrective based on first hand observation might be apt here. After my talks in North America and Europe where I presented research and interview data about my book *Syrian Women Refugees* (2019a), more often than not, I would receive questions about Syrian women's mosque visits as a socializing strategy in a foreign country. The audience assumed that I could reach more women to interview if I had access to the mosques and attended prayers. I realized that they equated mosque attendance with weekly church visits, which is problematic to say the least. Searching for a mosque in their new country is not common among practicing Muslim women since this is not something that they would do back home. In fact, the household can be the primary locus of religious socialization for most Muslim refugee women (Silvestri 2011, 1231).

The data by Beaman, Selby, and Barras confirm that for most Muslims Canadians, "a mosque is unnecessary" and "*ad hoc* solutions are commonplace" (2017, 83). I cannot agree more with their statement that the "take me to your imam" approach is "a reconfiguration of the Christian imaginary of how religion works: a priest or pastor, often male, is imbued with social and religious authority" which does not translate as simply (83). Moreover, Beaman, Selby, and Barras warn that the stereotype of "the oppressed Muslim woman" still has a large presence in the public imaginary which often seems to override evidence to the contrary. The selections from their interviews with Syrian newcomers in Canada demonstrate that an overemphasis on mosque, prayer needs, and halal food stores may not reflect what refugees need (92).

Turaeva whose work is on mosque-attending migrant Muslim women in Moscow, perceptively underlines that "some, both women and men, prefer to practice their religion at home" and quotes from a Tadjik woman who has never attended a mosque in Moscow. She has better living conditions than an average migrant so she doesn't belong to the "imagined community" who seek "for opportunities and safety which can be found in the mosque" (2019, 141). The self-identified Muslim women whom I interviewed for this book don't attend or seek mosques in their host countries either.

Maritato's study on women and Islam in contemporary Turkey concludes that "in everyday life, inviting women to mosques requires the vaize to be aware of the communities' heterogeneous attendance" (2020, 31). Inviting women to participate in the mosques is nothing but an effort to forge a "new religious woman" who represents these old, traditional models in a modern way (31). This attempt can be applied to many mosques outside of Turkey, and presents itself as yet another reason for why the Syrian women whom I interviewed haven't sought out mosques. They are more innovative, eclectic, and independent in their interpretations and practices of Islam than what the traditional models aim to mold in a mosque. Instead of looking only at public Islamic places, addressing attention to different spaces such as households and their changing nature may allow scholars to see a different face of Islam and different process of Islamization as McDaugall suggests (2008).

In order to reframe and resolve the continuous challenge of accommodation for Muslims' rights and how to make Islam fit the dominant policies of religious governance in Denmark (and Europe in general), Jørgen S. Nielsen suggested thinking critically of churchification, but he produced work solely on the integration of *organised* Muslim life into western European states (my emphasis). In "Churchification of Islam in Europe," Niels Vinding criticizes partial and problematic approach to Islam in Europe, building on Nielsen's work. Assuming that mosques are like churches is a "misrecognition" on many levels "in Islam and Muslim organizations" (2018, 64) and acting on such a misrecognition will "at best yield no result, at worst do irreversible damage to state and religion relations" and complicates integration efforts. I share these scholars' concerns; yet, they are missing the unmeasurable alternatives, the already-integrated Muslims who have been keen to remain out of this political power game of churchification in Europe and also in North America as the audience of my talks revealed. The Syrian women's voices in this book are evidence to it.

Amina Nayel's ethnographic study, conducted with Sudanese women immigrants in the U.K. with a strong emphasis on intersectionality, is another substantial work on Muslim women migrants. Nayel attempts to encompass gender, class, ethnicity, nationality and religion (Islam) in her analysis of multiple inequalities. The regimes of inequality that are observed in West Yorkshire resonate with the categories of difference that relate to Sudanese women, as African, Muslim, and migrant. The book challenges not only the "homogenous categories of Muslims in the U.K." but also analyzes "the interplay between gender and other forms of power and difference with a feminist lens" and reveals "the impact of the diaspora space on the women's agency" (2017, 23).

Mandaville conducted another study in the U.K. with the British-born youth in the context of an heightened intra-Islamic pluralism of the diaspora, which is increasingly valorized by Muslims in Europe. Mandaville argues that the younger generation is largely "dissatisfied with the Islam of their parents" (2001, 121) and highly skeptical about the authorities like imams "to rearticulate the Islamic tradition in the vernacular language" (124). Not surprisingly, the result is the emergence of youth associations as new places of transmission and reflection on Islamic knowledge that accompany or complement individualized practices, the lived Islam. To briefly note a distinction that I came across during my research on definitions is the difference that Nyhage and Halsaa made between lived religion and individualized religion. They argue against their interchangeable use; rather, individualized religion can be part of lived religion (2016, 39).

Kuppinger's ethnographic fieldwork is a remarkable example of lived religion conducted in a working class/immigrant neighborhood of Stuttgart. It illustrates the workings of informal Muslim religious authority, women's casual negotiations of everyday Muslim practices and sensitivities in informal moments and spaces (2020). Women seek to inform their peers as unofficial religious authorities about best possible pious practices during which authority does not work in a top-down manner. Transferring Deeb's study from the Lebanese context to Germany, Kuppinger too illustrates that lived religion takes place in "streets, on balconies, in cafés, kitchens […], at women's morning meetings and men's evening conversation, and with families sitting around the television at night" (Deeb 2006, 101).

Kuppinger's point that the lived application of theological knowledge in women's daily lives is more complex than the selective contexts of mosques is complementary to the above examples regarding the mosque-attendance criterion when considering women's religiosities. Because of their ephemeral and random nature, informal encounters that Kuppinger and Deeb refer to are harder to observe and chronicle than discussions in a Qur'an course taking place in women's quarters of a mosque. Nevertheless, they are significant aspects of religious, social, and cultural negotiations and transformations that deserve further academic investigation. These daily, non-hierarchical reflections of Islam are more likely to remain unnoticed unless lived religion is developed further theoretically and methodologically.

In their inquiry on the lack of Muslim voices, Friedmann Marquardt et al. raise intriguing questions such as: "Is it perhaps harder or riskier for Muslims to voice their concerns in the public sphere about any issue when many are simply trying to avoid any attention, most of which tends to be negative?" (2013, 285). I don't discard the possibility of a strategic avoidance of being at the forefront of protests, and I agree with the authors that more research needs to be undertaken into the advocacy of non-Christian FBOs around the issue of undocumented migration or asylum seeking (284). However, I find their focus on FBOs and their definition of "voice" limited. It is exactly due to these institution-based approaches that non-organized Muslims' voices in the Global North have remained mostly unheard. Muslim refugee women's voices inevitably receive their share of this invisibility.

Studies on Muslim Women Refugees and Agency

When religion (particularly Islam) is analyzed in RFMS, the focus is heavily on the role of conflicts and politicized religious identities. The relationship between religious persecution and receiving asylum remains central both to the definition of refugee and asylee as well as to the scholarly debates on religion-refugeeism nexus. This attitude is one main reason for exclusion of women refugees' voices when it comes to collecting data on everyday religion and its link to resilience.

Gozdziak's works (2004; 2008) stand out as promising exceptions since they include discussions on gender and religion in the lives of refugee women. First, she acknowledges that refugee women's engagement with religion is "very different from the experiences of refugee men" (2008, 189). After citing several studies which demonstrated that men and women react differently when faced with similar hostile circumstances, Gozdziak provides an example from her fieldwork with the Muslim Kosovar Albanians at Fort Dix, New Jersey. She observed that after the weekly Friday (*Jumah*) prayers, the men stayed with the imam to talk about politics and speculated on the outcomes of the war whereas the women inquired about the facilities available for their children, planned for weddings and child-naming ceremonies for the babies born in the camp. Expressed in the affective style of Gozdziak, "the men prayed and looked back, while the women prayed and kept walking" (2008,189).

However, Gozdziak displays complexities through firsthand narratives of refugee women realistically. Her conclusion is that religion operates in competing and contradictory ways regarding the women's experiences as refugees, serving as a source of resiliency but also as an impediment of integration processes. Had she reframed some of her fieldwork within the lived religion and distinguished the women's quotidian practices among themselves, she would have generated more discussions on religion's constructive and practical effects on refugee women.

McMichael's findings on Somali Muslim women refugees in Melbourne are potentially pertinent as a pathway to my work with Syrian Muslim women except her polished conclusion. Despite her repeated acknowledgment of "many versions" of Islam (2002, 182, 187), she fails to designate Somali women's denominations (e.g., Sunni) and lists their material practices without reservations: attending mosques, buying meat at halal butchers, wearing veil, fast and feast during Ramadan, sending children to Islamic weekend schools, and visiting sheikhs for good fortune and during times of crisis (180). Valuable for its integration of Muslim women refugee voices in literature, her findings nevertheless contrast with my respondents' unsettling commentaries on their faith-based practices. To achieve more inclusivity and make non-organized Muslim women refugees visible as well, McMichael's ethnographic research needs to be reviewed by the notion of lived religion.

Secil Dagtas joins the criticism of policy makers in macro structures through the analysis of her interviews with 15 Syrian women in Hatay, Turkey (2018). Shifting her focus from institutional governance to women's everyday social relations (neighborliness, kinship, and hospitality), Dagtas argues that intersectional feminists can encapsulate the nuances of refugee women's agency better, and thus can challenge the current representations of victimized, suffering refugee women. Her warning against the pretext that the Muslim societies enforce sexual and religious subordination of women raises timely questions on justifying anti-immigrant rhetoric and border control in the Global North. In the Middle East (Turkey included), asylum laws and resettlement policies are less structured and more dependent on local practices than their Western counterparts. This fact may indeed provide displaced women to negotiate their social roles to their benefit. These acts take place mostly in women-only venues, "often within the home space" and as a result, Syrian women's daily interactions are rarely recorded or brought to the public and political debates in the Global North (51). Faith-based practices fall into these unpredictable acts and need analysis as I attempt to undertake here.

Mentioned earlier in the context of resilience and religiosity, Kanal and Rottmann's article on Syrian refugee women (2021) contributes also to Dagtas's criticism. Since their fieldwork "took place in women's homes," it is worth revisiting here (5). Their broader objective is "to prompt a re-thinking of refugee women's everyday agency for scholars researching migration" to provide better support for the displaced women in their daily lives. It also demonstrates Kanal and Rottmann's frustration with "the image of passive 'womenandchildren'" (1). I join them in their call for an "interdisciplinary discussion of a cultural and gender sensitive theory of agency" as an urgent need in academia (11). I value their "more comprehensive approach to agency," especially regarding Islamic coping strategies (e.g., patience and acceptance of one's conditions) which may seem to keep women "from changing their situation" on the surface (11).

However, Kanal and Rottmann argue that when coping strategies lead to women's psychological health and wellbeing rather than "changing social structures" as the more mainstream approach to agency indicates, then coping can provide an effective framework for theories of agency (11).

Similarly, Ruba Salih's study of Palestinian refugee women's agency by focusing on "the ordinary, the domestic, bodily vulnerability and grief" challenges the "modern political paradigms of the subject" where agency in the public sphere is the only intelligible way to act (2017, 756). This awareness on the gender-specific silences will help researchers to avoid producing incomplete or misleading knowledge in academia. Meredith McGuire's reminder is telling here that "humans are creative agents, not merely oversocialized automatons" and the faith-practices that people strategically adopt to shape their experiences are often "completely unforeseen by the official religion" (2008, 98). I endeavor to discover, record, and disseminate the unforeseen not only in this work but also in the future.

Ghorashi's approach to women's agency via what she refers to as "engaged narrative methodology" is in line with the studies that are addressed here, particularly with Kanal and Rottmann's. This means considering agency in terms of "small changes that are taken up by individuals, groups, communities, academia and so on, in their daily reflective actions" (2021, 59). She brings forth the concept of micro-emancipation, less grandiose and more focused than in older conceptualizations of agency, which is rather "partial, temporal movements breaking away from diverse forms of oppression rather than moving towards" (59).

"(Ir)Reconcilable Identities" is worthy of acknowledgement as an exceptional study. It is the only research to my knowledge that is undertaken to understand the role of religion in the lives of LGBTQ refugees from Islamic societies before flight, during forced migration, and into early resettlement (Alessi et al. 2019). Conducted in Austria and the Netherlands, the excerpts from the interviews demonstrate a remarkable plurality in navigating one's religious identity, that is, ranging from a rejection of organized religion, drawing strength from one's faith to reclaiming Islam in one's own way. I mention the article here due to its temporal inclusivity of the topic; namely, before, during and after the experience of displacement and flight via lived religion.

Finally, caution must be exercised with studies conducted with Muslim women who reside in Europe. Because these studies subtly suggest that female adherents of Islam become more egalitarian and liberated as a result of moving to the Global North, and not because of the religion or the cultural history itself. Unlike some other Eurocentric scholars such as Cesari who claims "the normative Islamic tradition transforms and dissolves as Muslim minorities settle and 'a Muslim individual' emerges" (2003, 259), Mandaville attributes any principal forces of change not to Europe or the West, but "to the effects of travel and migration." In his work, the transformation of Islam happens "in a translocal space" where the political community of the host society is not always accepted or embraced (2001, 105). In this regard, studying Syrian women's religio-spiritual strategies and how they are empowered by them in non-western contexts become even more significant. Rania Kamla's article in the Syrian context (2018) and the transregional study of Merin Shobhana Xavier's book chapter (2021) regarding the Sufi women leaders are among the examples that counter the implied notion of gender egalitarianism of Islam once it is moved to the West. Anna M. Gade's warning on limitations of secular perspectives in current English language academic settings of environmental humanities can be applied also to lived religion as a valuable cautionary (2019).

CHAPTER IV

THE INTERVIEWS

The Interviewing Process

There are two metaphors to describe contradictory epistemological conceptions, the interviewer as a miner, the interviewer as a traveler (Kvale and Brinkmann 2009, 48-49). The mining metaphor assumes a static view of knowledge, while the travel metaphor acknowledges new knowledge production and the possibility that the traveler/researcher might transform during the journey. Epistemologically, I adopt the travel metaphor, which offers an "understanding of knowledge as something being produced, interpreted and constructed" where the mining metaphor has a positivistic stance, implying that knowledge is waiting to be discovered (Bremborg 2011, 311).

The initial challenge I faced when I began the research was to meet the women in person and gain their trust to record their narratives of disruption, loss, and displacement among other themes. The Syrian activist Muzna Dureid who had confidence in my research was an important conduit of my legitimization among the women with whom she put me in touch. She was an essential bridge and reference for my initiation into most of the Syrian women whom I interviewed. I also owe to Nilgün Yıldırım, staff at an NGO which provides psychosocial and legal support for refugees in Istanbul for connecting me to two Syrian women for my earlier work (Ezer 2019a; 2020) since one of them features in this book as well. Secil Erdogan Ertorer teaching in Toronto at the time introduced me to two Syrians, one of whom agreed to interview.

The extensive literature on conducting oral histories rarely pays attention to how the already complex power dynamics of the interview are further complicated by the introduction of an interpreter. It can force the interviewer to share authority, cede control or it prevents discussions from developing organically. This is the main reason why I chose participants who were generally fluent if not proficient in English and did not require a translator to interpret our conversations with the exception of Lutfia.

The initial exchange prior to the interview took place exclusively in the form of email correspondences, and switched to either text or free messaging apps. My electronic "Project Information" document had the following items:

1. The purpose and scope of the project (its intended outcomes, end product -the book-, duration of the project, how it is funded);

2. My contact details and a short resume listing my qualifications and affiliations;

3. What I looked for in narrator profiles (their background, contribution, motivations etc.);

4. What narrators can expect from me (confidentiality, practicalities of interviews, that they won't be paid, but any expenses will be covered);

5. The legal parameters and protections around any information that I am provided (such as data protection, copyright, archiving, future access, possible publishing venues, etc.)

The interviews were conducted mostly in cafes, and only once continued in the temporary household of one respondent in Athens. We had no immediate safety concerns but I urged the respondents to keep their names and identity confidential. I also highlighted the benefits of making the personal political in my work, and shared my stance transparently with the respondents. Displaying my position, vulnerability, and involvement in the project was essential for the organic development of the interview process and how accounts were recorded.

My position was of an insider-outsider, being from the Middle East Region which was further complicated by my advanced level of English with a slight American accent, and almost two decades of living abroad, which continues to be a mark of prestige for the women I interviewed. My hybrid status (privilege of international mobility/travel via the U.S. citizenship) might have complicated the question of belonging in their minds but it was not brought to their attention. I wondered whether the interlocutors viewed me as a safer alternative to another woman within their community of Syrians or someone from the Global North when sharing their stories and ideas. Whenever we conversed, we arrived at an imaginary, fuzzy, generously cultured and layered area where Middle Eastern and Western facets overlapped.

There is also the dialogical nature of narration that is shaped during the interviewing, which extends beyond the interview setting to wider imagined audiences. This informs the sensitivities of both the interviewer and her respondents about what can be addressed easily, what is more delicate or better avoided altogether in regard to individualized Islamic practices.

Moreover, to "give voice" to women's own words will "always only be partial" considering that it is the researcher who designs the interview format and decides for the excerpt selection to quote or comment on (Buitelaar 2020,14). However, this limitation can be overcome by working with a small number of research participants with whom one decides together what to take out or edit as I practiced earlier (Ezer 2017; 2019a) and here as well.

The transcription process was smooth, I asked about the unclear parts and sent the respondents the transcriptions as word files in gently edited English. It was upon their request that the grammar and vocabulary get modified during my process of typing the interviews. Depending on the goals of the project and prior commitments, Hoffman recommends that transcribing can be the best practice in traditional oral history and the archiving of it. For instance, if the end product will be a written document, she recommends typing out all or deciding whether transcribing the whole interview is worth it as a background product of the project. People can deposit their material in an official archive that requires full transcription as well as audio formats, and if the final product will be in audio or video format, all interviews' transcription into text may not be necessary (Hoffman 2020, 152).

After acknowledging knowledge as construed and constructed, my stance is that the narratives on faith-based commitments and practices are not simply tools to make claims on the truth of women's experience. Rather, the interviews were a reciprocal opportunity for me and the respondents to explore how Syrian women maintain resilience and order in their lives during the post-2011 period. Their interpretations of Islam as lived religion were meaningful at the time of sharing and that is what mattered the most. Religious concepts spread beyond metaphysical contexts as we spoke and were embodied in a range of emotional and moral experiences. The women also demonstrated that identities are always multistrand and intersectional, and that faith-based practices are some of the many components of an individual. Not all were believers of God, yet they reflected upon Islam, religions in general or generated spiritualities that were free of God.

There were also silences around specific experiences such as not to speak of the war in detail. Instead, some women moved from pre-war Syria narratives to their arrival in the host country, while others described the war as a series of events, entailing generalizations without emotional edge. I accepted silences within narratives out of respect for women's faith and integrity. I also acknowledge silence as "spaces" which enabled some women to construct their narratives in meaningful and adequate ways (Stringer 2013, 170).

The Profiles of 13 Syrian Women

To preserve confidentiality and safety, some of the women's names have been changed and some were comfortable with the first-name use except Muzna Dureid who also featured on the cover of my book (2019). Despite sharing a refugee status, even the briefest summaries as in below demonstrate the diversity in women's backgrounds.

Lutfia (52) is from Dara, married with three children. She lives in Istanbul with her husband, children, and her in-laws. She is a practicing Sunni-Muslim, took the hijab after marriage. She volunteers at an NGO to improve the conditions of Syrian children's education in Turkey, finds solace in reading the Quran in hard times.

Muzna (30) is from Aleppo, single, raised as Muslim, but lost her faith after 2011. She is a well-known human rights activist with a degree in French linguistics. We met in Istanbul in June 2016 where the interview took place. Upon a grant from Nobel Women's Initiative, she went to Ottawa, and lives in Montreal as of 2021 with her family who joined her a year ago. She is the liaison officer for the White Helmets, and an MA student at Concordia University.

Emilia (32) is from Homs, single, raised by a Muslim single mother with four older brothers. She was a high-school dropout, however, the World University Service of Canada offered her a university placement in Toronto in 2014. She completed her major in Political Science in 2018. Her faith journey was from a practicing believer to an atheist-agnostic.[6]

Sama (32) arrived in Germany with her parents and sister in 2015. She has a degree in Translation. She was raised a Sunni Muslim, wears the hijab, and enjoys regular conversations about Islam and its history with her family. Religion is an important part of her identity. In December 2018, she got married to Syrian engineer in Darmstadt, also a practicing Muslim. They had a daughter in 2021.

Zizinia (41) is from Aleppo, a single mother with two daughters. She has a degree in Economics. Currently, she lives and works in Gaziantep, Turkey. She was raised Muslim in a liberal family and went to a private Jesuit school, monitored by the government. She took the hijab for two years (2015-2017). Her faith practices fluctuate but are creative and energizing.

Leila (30) is from Deir Ez-Zor with a degree in environmental engineering. We met in Istanbul in 2017 and she moved to Montreal (Canada) in January 2019. She was raised Muslim, with a non-practicing

---

[6] Rakı is made of distilled grapes and anise, and considered the national alcoholic drink of Turkey.

mother and an atheist father. Her faith practices fluctuate but sustains her in difficult times. She got married in April 2021, and is attending Concordia University.

Sara (29) is from Latakia, was born into a conservative Alawite Muslim family. She studied pharmacy instead of literature due to parental pressure, left Syria in December 2015, currently lives and works in Athens. Her father's lineage as a sheik made him a respectable religious figure but also a very strict person. Sara's faith journey was from a practicing Muslim teenager to an atheist-agnostic.

Bidaa (36) is a lawyer from Aleppo. She grew up in a close-knit Sunni Muslim family where the mother is the boss. She was living in Athens at the time of our interviews, then married to a Syrian man in Germany and moved there. As a devout Muslim, Bidaa makes extra efforts to dismantle the stereotypes about Islam and women, likes debating with her non-Muslim friends. She had a daughter in 2020.

Ola (45) is from Damascus with a high-school diploma. She grew up with her sisters and a communist-atheist father, and calls herself an atheist. She has experimented with a few faith communities in Syria with no success. She is a single mother with two children. She sought asylum in Canada in 2017 and her children joined her in Vancouver in March 2019. She completed the Social Service Worker diploma program in April 2021.

Lubna (40) is a women's rights activist working at an NGO in Turkey at the time of the interview (February 2020). Originally from Ghouta (east of central Damascus), she grew up in a liberal Sunni family, and had to leave the university due to the war during her graduation year. She recently graduated from The Academic University for Non-violence and Human Rights based in Lebanon known as Aunohre. She is married and has a son. She moved to France with her family in 2022.

Muna (36) is a pharmacist, grew up in a Sunni family with practicing parents who even completed their Mecca pilgrimage. She has an MS in congestive heart failure. She is a survivor of the chemical attack in Eastern Ghouta but lost her brother, who was also her best friend. She received a grant and moved to London for graduate studies (Global Health and Conflict) at St. George's University in late 2020.

Dima (31) is a graduate of Political Science from a private university in Istanbul. She is the recipient of the Young Change Maker Award of 2019. She held several jobs such as in MTN (mobile phone operator company in Syria), radio station, and Orient Policy Center among others. She is a self-proclaimed human rights activist and digital security person with intentions of becoming a journalist.

Rawan (40) holds a BA in Biology from Aleppo University, is working for Vancouver Association for Survivors of Torture (VAST) as an intake and interpreter staff since 2019. She was born into a Sunni Muslim family and was practicing until her mid-twenties. She did volunteer work in Lebanon in 2017 before applying for asylum in Canada. Her work experience ranges from being a lab expert to teaching biology for ten years in a high school in Aleppo.

All respondents are either strongly anti-government or expressed anti-government tendencies at some point during the interviews. Except for two respondents, the interviewees regularly referred to the events of 2011 as "the Revolution" which I used only once without the brackets, that is, of my own choice. They had to leave Syria after 2011, except Emilia who decided earlier that her life plans didn't match her family and society's. I stand in full support of the respondents' decisions under the circumstances at the time and acknowledge with them that a near future return to Syria is considered very unlikely. The history and the analysis of the Syrian conflict (how it began, spread, and evolved over the past 10 years) is beyond the limits of this study, and the amount of resources are plenty and accessible for any reader who is interested.

The Setting and the Dynamics

Establishing a safe space for the interviews was part of my feminist stance and methodology, that is, making the experience of sharing life stories with difficult knowledge also fulfilling and nurturing. I always arrived earlier to our meeting place, and tried to secure a quiet and cozy spot in cafés. After the participant's arrival and exchanging greetings, I made sure to check about the seat arrangement, ordered hot or cold drinks and snacks at her choice before I took out my phone/recorder and assumed the interviewer's role. Although it was already stated in my introductory email to them, I reminded both of us to relinquish the idea of following a specific plan of *my* own making. I strongly believe that creating this space of hospitality contributed to the success of the interviews, the depth, and the intimacy in the answers that I received. A reciprocal bonding was also embodied in the manner that we parted (kissing and/or hugging) after each meeting and our follow-up phone texts and emails.

Paying attention to the details in conducting interviews is part of what Christie Neuger labels "deconstructive listening," which I include within mindful listening methods. Careful listening to women's stories allows "opportunities to subvert the control of oppressive personal stories" (2001,

90-92). The Syrian women and I forged several moments of cultural (in particular, culinary) and religio-spiritual alliances derived from our everyday lives as two conversing women. Even the thickness of Turkish coffee had the potential to serve as an embodied intimacy that seemed to affect the conventional dynamics of interviewing positively.

I don't claim that these cultural affinities dissolved the power imbalance inherent in the interview situations in general, but in most cases at least, they reduced social distance. My construction of the interviews was intentionally against any possible exploitative nature of conventional and asymmetrical interviewing. This meant that the consent forms included statements that allowed the respondent full access to the transcriptions and the option to edit them before my presentations or publications. They could pull out from the project at any phase which happened only once at an early stage in Sweden. My determination on reducing the power dynamics to the minimum possible demanded longer hours of work and caused constant stress of losing a narrative unexpectedly.

Reciprocality and transparency that I discussed in the section on my position as a researcher bring about the concept of hospitality, "clearly a virtue in the ethical sense" and "an act of kindness, an act of love in the general sense" (Carrière 2017, 153). The experience of hospitality was a shared one in the sense that the countries (with the exception of Turkey) that I visited for the interviews issued the residency to them first, and I was there only temporarily. Syrian culture values hospitality highly as all Middle Eastern societies. The initiative of someone who offers hospitality to a woman-on-the-move is a "substitute for the deficiencies of the state which, in the case of asylum seekers, rarely fulfils the obligations it has undertaken by signing international conventions." However, as an engaged scholar, I perceive shared hospitality also "a kind of resistance, a resistance to feelings" of suspicion or fear that affect the decisions and practices of the researcher and the interviewee (153).

My attitude was occasionally criticized by some of my colleagues whose congenial advice was on favoring my time and labor. However, their comments also demonstrated mainstream arrangements and expectations in academia regarding the interview process. Locating the issue of authority in her discussion on the relationship of the researcher-researched, Susan Geiger encourages honesty about the limitations of the relation and seeks mutual respect against the existing gaps between two people (1990, 175). She radically refers to the respondents as "the oral historian" throughout her article, and remains skeptical of the bonds ("fictive relational assertions") that can be established during interviews. The reason for her distrust is that the constructed links might bring not just benefits or empathy but also obligations that accompany these fictive bonds (176). While acknowledging Geiger's concerns, I didn't get the feeling that calling each other sister or *habibti* imposed expectations during or after my interviews. However, assuming mother/daughter or aunty roles would be more likely to raise issues.

I share Sprague's critique on conventional ways of reporting findings that create "the effect of hiding the researcher," thus, I attempted to practice and promote reflectivity throughout (2005, 22). This endeavor promotes a relational agency and transparency for both parties as well as the readers of this book. Increasing the likelihood of posing critical questions becomes possible by developing a relationship with the interviewee on interpersonal grounds, which enables researchers to move "outside of our closed academic conversations" (182-188). I consider this relationship not as a static but a fluid, transparent, and layered bond. Once again, it promotes a relational agency for the researcher, the interlocutor, and the reader, reminding me of Orsi's reference to the Sartrean definition of what research is: "a relationship between human beings" (qtd. in Orsi 2005, 174).

The relationship between the researcher/writer and the respondent is and will remain delicate and complex, particularly when the feminist methodologies and stances are claimed. Ann Oakley's reminder that "negotiating publications with research participants generated sporadic discussion, especially in feminist academic circles" still remains meaningful and pertinent here, but also as "one of the unsolved methodological and ethical issues" regarding research (2016, 208). This was confirmed through the criticism that I received for establishing friendships with some of my respondents and for not demonstrating a proud ownership of the end products (the book, articles, public talks) after my work with Syrian women refugees was completed.

Oakley's point on building friendship during and post-interview periods stimulates an intriguing discussion from a feminist viewpoint of which I am a proponent. I partake in her experience that "friendship is not a simple or unitary phenomenon in any context" because friendships, "overlapping with other types of social connection such as kinship and community," can become a component of the interviewing process (2016, 209). Therefore, the concept of friendship and its applicability to interview relations may require more exploration in oral history and qualitative research. Oakley offers the notion of "gift" in the form of vignettes about "resilience and coping, about struggle and success" as a "fruitful framework for understanding" (208-209). The interdependence of researchers and participants who agreed to contribute through their memories and life stories can indeed be worded as generous sharing/gifting. In this context, I encourage RFMS scholars whose research include interviews to investigate also the flourishing studies on conceptualizing friendship between citizens and refugees in addition to the researcher-interlocutor relationship (Häberlen 2016; Simich and Andermann 2014). These two studies are outside of feminist paradigms but nevertheless valuable and interrelated from my perspective.

That women's agency and empowerment can be located in piety and in the right to choose submission challenge feminist liberal conceptions of what agency or empowerment is. My view is that key feminist concepts of autonomy and freedom should not serve to further dichotomies since they are inseparable from relationships and interdependence among women or other structural factors in any society. Following Orsi, I argue that attention must be paid to the structures and conditions in which any form of agency or empowerment is performed including what is built and shared between the narrator/interlocutor and the researcher.

Mary E. Hunt (1991) maps a path from unjust, unequal power relationships imposed by external circumstances to new experiences of mutuality through women's friendship via a combination of case studies, first-person accounts, and literary sources. Informed thoroughly by intertextuality, she charts new theological and socio-ethical interpretations for friendship. She presents a convincing argument that when women opt for living in gynocentric interactions, compelling paradigms of the holy emerge, shaped by elements of mutual influence, co-responsibility, and commitment on the divine-human equation. This is a view from a feminist theological perspective which I have felt an affinity to but didn't share it with the respondents due to their varied faith histories.

My experiences with the Syrian women confirm Marella Hoffman's conclusion that every refugee narrator does "a very good job on the spot of regulating, editing and navigating for themselves how much they want to tell you or can tell you" (2020, 100). Nevertheless, Hoffman offers a thorough list on the "levels of common sense" regarding the interviews. Some examples are: 1. Always respecting refugees' hierarchy of needs, 2. Managing refugee narrators' expectations of what the researcher can achieve for them, 3. Doing one's best to ensure that the resources that a refugee narrator invests in the interview (at a minimum, their time, energy, trust, emotions, and memory) will return proportional benefits to them in at least some way. Providing the sense that they are part of a positive project and that they receive honesty, respect, and quality listening throughout the process is significant (101-103).

Discussing emotions among oral history practitioners should not be avoided or depreciated. In fact, it needs to be extended to other fields such as Refugee and Forced Migration Studies. Talking about the women's feelings but keeping my internal realm private did not seem fair or sustainable. Conversing on one's faith history and religio-spiritual practices requires emotional disclosure, open-heartedness, and sensitivity so demanding objectivity from the researcher herself, is neither ethical nor feasible as feminist researchers have already noted (Bondi 2005; Munt 2012; Oakley 2016). Hence, I was prepared to answer personal questions when the occasion arose. This rarely happened since the women were enthusiastic about talking about their personal experiences, articulating themselves, and thus construing a voice of their own. They entrusted the editorial responsibilities to me, requesting that I correct English mistakes as I compose their narratives. Thus, I have resumed the role of the author-editor since I did not and will not be using their words without their final consent.

I share the anticipation with Streib et al. that the notion of lived religion can be understood as an "open space for a broader theological discussion" (2008, xii). Through Syrian women refugees' voices on faith-based practices and beliefs, I intend to expand innovative dialogues across multiple disciplines over time (particularly in RFMS). The current literature will benefit from these genuine accounts. After all, living religio-spiritual practices are shaped by the "readiness of migrants to negotiate with outsiders and cope with the limitations of their context." In addition, their "ability to develop effective tactics for addressing the challenges of migration and the requirement to integrate" are also part of this formation (Knott 2016, 86).

The selected passages of women in the following chapter illustrate the complexity of religio-spiritual concerns, beliefs, and opinions through various examples of lived religion. They contribute to the literature on how women relate to building and/or maintaining resilience, exceeding, reconfiguring, and negotiating the boundaries of religions (Ai et al. 2003; Eppsteiner and Hagan 2016; McMichael 2002; Pargament 1997; Shaw and Joseph 2005). Their main context is the boundaries of the official Islam in Syria as imposed by religious authorities while tackling their own realities and interpretations throughout their journeys as displaced individuals.

CHAPTER VI

THE SELECTIONS FROM SYRIAN WOMEN'S LIVED ISLAM IN SURVIVING DISPLACEMENT AND TRAUMA

Among the respondents' rich interpretive flora of diversity in Islam, five themes can be identified and processed through the concept of lived religion. The first relates to the workings of the Quran as an empowerment tool during the extended periods of distress and ambiguity (particularly in the accounts by Lutfia, Zizinia, Leila, Sama, and Bidaa). The second is the faith and resilience link; whether believers might be better equipped to overcome trauma as refugees and develop personal strengths differently from non-believers (as in the accounts of Lutfia, Zizinia, Leila, Sama, and Bidaa versus Sara, Emilia, Ola, and Muna). Faith and resilience relationship is discussed along with post traumatic growth (PTG) by comparing the respondents' statements on God, Islam, spirituality, and inner strength. The third is women's reformulating the efforts of adaptation to a new country as a form of worship in Islam, that is, "work as a spiritual practice/ora at labora" (McGuire 2008, 109) as can be observed in the accounts of Zizinia, Bidaa, Sama, and Lutfia in particular. This proves to be challenging to separate from the second, and it can emerge as a sub-theme as well in my study.

The fourth theme relates to a body modification, that is, getting tattoos, which was not considered unacceptable or inappropriate for several respondents against the common belief that they are disapproved in Islam. On the contrary, tattoos provide women a form of permanency and resilience regarding their religio-spirituality (e.g., tattooing Allah in Arabic) at times and serve as reminders of various events, places or people. Finally, five pillars of Islam, the "so-called 'essence of Islam' is no longer or has never been fully in practice nor submitted to without reservations" and they can "differ and has differed according to the time and location of the Muslims being observed" (Reinhart 2020, 6). The following passages are indeed confirming and complementary evidence to Reinhart's study on lived Islam. My years of research and many interviews have indicated that the only undisputed pillar is the profession of faith known as *shahada* (there is no god but God, and Muhammad is the Messenger of God) as mentioned in the accounts of Zizinia, Rawan, Muna, Lubna, Dima, and Leila.

For the women above, religion has been a meaning-maker, providing each of them with a sense of meaning in the world. It has served as a foothold and foundation in their displaced lives and under the contingent conditions, which they use to interpret and understand the world (e.g., Zizinia and Rawan) while for others religion has a more taken-for-granted aspect that can be compartmentalized and drawn upon in times of need (e.g., Leila and Lubna). Religion also has a communal component and as such provides individuals with social identities, that comes with a strong sense of belonging to a community and opportunities for citizenship practices depending on the host country conditions. However, the aspect of belonging or identity is not without reservations, especially for single refugee women as some of their accounts attest.

Lutfia whose marital problems in Syria were aggravated by sharing the same household with her in-laws in Istanbul finds solace in regular readings of and listening to the Quran: "Thank Allah that I am more knowledgeable about Islam now than in my twenties, and reading the Quran is my main guidance and consolation. When I feel down, I seek refuge in the verses of the Quran. I hope I will never forget praying or the Quranic verses since they are the most valuable for me" (Ezer 2019a, 49).

Similar to the other interviewees, Lutfia's discomfort about responding to the questions on spirituality subsided as soon as the questions about God and Islam were posed:

> In Syria, I used to have a garden which I enjoyed tending to, and it would tend to my soul in return. Whenever I watered the plants and sat down with a cup of coffee in my hand, I felt as if I transcended of this world. Is it spirituality? (....) In Istanbul, when I sit by the coast and watch the sea and the seagulls, I forget all about this life and its issues. However, there is always something pulling me out of it, several responsibilities are waiting for me. I don't know how to expand on these moments further; maybe it is better not to answer. (49)

Lutfia's reluctance for further exploring her feelings of transcendence doesn't make her statements less valuable than the ones on Islam. Bonding with nature clearly stirs some form of the extraordinariness in her that is captured by Soelle's definition of spirituality, "knowledge of God through and from experience" (2001, 45) which I integrate into the unsystematic nature of lived religion to enrich the discussion on refugees' experiences, following Streib's proposal (2008, 54).

Lutfia is knowledgeable about the Quran to the extent that she quoted *ayats* by heart during our conversations, aptly contextualizing the lines such as her displacement or war in Syria: "No misfortune can happen, either in the earth or in yourselves, that was not set down in writing before We brought it into being" (Quran 57: 22). She repeated more than once that her "inner strength comes from God" to keep her stamina against the verbal and psychological harassment that she was subjected to by her in-laws. Whenever tension builds up at home and "we are about to burst, I listen to the Quran and feel that God calms down the whole house and grants me some peace" (Ezer 2019a, 49) is another powerful statement that Lutfia made regarding the healing effects of her sacred book.

As a younger and single refugee, Leila's connection to the Quran and how she relates to the selected *ayats* during challenging times were also actualized on several occasions. As an example of lived religion, one of her integrations of Quranic prayer to daily life is a yellow post-it note next to her mirror at home in Istanbul: "I posted a line from the Quran (94: 6), 'Fa Inna Ma al 'usri Yusra' (Truly, where there is hardship, there is also ease). This line from Sura *Al-Inshirah* (Relief, solace) gives me hope and instills the belief in me that after some challenges in life, relief will follow with the help of Allah" (Ezer 2019a,125). Leila's comments on Islam and that she doesn't recognize herself as a Muslim in the traditional sense is evidence for the necessity of expanding debates on lived religion. She expressed several times that she is a believer but only if appearance did not matter:

> I'd consider myself a good Muslim and someone who is devoted to God in her own way, because I don't hurt anyone and I treat people kindly. I may not be fasting or praying five times a day, but I sometimes read passages from the Quran, talk to God, and recite some prayers. There are a lot of people who fast or dress conservatively, but they may not be good Muslims when you look inside their hearts. (125)

Similar passages can be found in other Syrian women's interpretations of themselves in the context of Muslim women. Zizinia is another example: "The main principles that I believe are that there is one God, there is an end to this life, and there is an afterlife. You need to serve other people in ethical and kind ways. This world is not only about you; instead, you are a servant on this earth" (103). By using almost the same words uttered by Lutfia whose appearance is more conservative with a headscarf and loose-fitting clothing, Zizinia, with her dyed hair and elaborate eye makeup around her large blue eyes, underlines the significance of the Quran in her life: "The Quran is the only book which I truly love and am knowledgeable about its chapters and certain passages by heart. Normally, I can't remember a book even on the second day after finishing it, but the Quran is a big exception" (103).

Without making a direct connection unlike Lutfia, Zizinia expresses the source of her stamina under the harsh circumstances in the following: "You won't succeed in this world unless you are spiritually strong. This is something that I still can't manage to put into words, but I know how to embrace and practice it in my life" (103). Considering that Zizinia doesn't pray in the prescribed manner, her confidence in the statement "I know how to embrace and practice it in my life" is a superb example to Islam as lived religion through the lenses of a Syrian woman who witnessed the discrepancy between the official and lived Islam early in life (103).

Zizinia is one of the two women who took the hijab for a while during her service in humanitarian work in a conservative area near the Turkish-Syrian border. In fact, at the first interview, she still wore a headscarf and by the time we finished the interviews, she did not. In hindsight, she cannot pinpoint the exact motive that led her into this decision but it wasn't only for the external forces, or in her gentle and poetic wording, for "having a passport to their [locals] hearts and gaining their respect." After a long pause, further retrospective accounts follow: "It was also a strange and cruel time for me. Finding the right words to capture my feelings is very hard. I hated myself for obeying a life despite myself, and this created a conflict and hatred in me" (105).

Zizinia began working at the border towns of the conflict immediately after her plane landed in Turkey from the U.S. where she spent nine months waiting for her asylum application to be processed in 2013. She took the hijab on the plane as the descent announcement was made. The alienation Zizinia felt in the U.S. despite the welcome of other Syrian expats and the financial aid from her uncle was aggravated by the longing for her two daughters. She received no support in her circle of friends and family when she announced her decision to return to Turkey, settle in there, and be close to Syria where people in need and her parents still live. Always a hardworking and independent woman who made her own living, the life as an asylum seeker in the U.S. was unbearable for her. Although she lacked the words for that "strange and cruel time," dependency on others and being unable to work officially must have triggered intruding thoughts leading to depression and confusion in the U.S. regardless of her financial situation. In this context, reconceptualizing one's religio-spiritual beliefs and practices is anticipated.

Zizinia lived and worked in Istanbul and Gaziantep after reuniting with her daughters whose impressive English and Turkish are demonstrated in our lively conversations and texting. She spent a total of 45 days in Syria in 2014, visited Membesh, an area where ISIS was trying to control then, and went to Aleppo. In fact, the circumstances were challenging to deal with psychologically: The U.S., Turkey, and Syria, none of which felt like home.

When I asked Zizinia about her practices of Islam, her car seat was the last place I would consider a space for a Muslim woman's worship. Everyday religion, however, "may happen in unpredictable places" and "may present itself to the observer as a question or puzzle whose meaning must be negotiated" (Ammerman 2007, 9). If stuck in the notorious Istanbul traffic when Zizinia heard of *ezan* (the call for prayer from the minarets) or knew that it was time for one of the daily prayers (namaz/salah), she wouldn't delay it, and recite the prayers quietly on the wheel, visualizing the movements in order. Driving is like meditation for her, she has felt at home in her car since she was a teenager.

Zizinia argues that the times are different now: One can take daily morning showers and spend the day by a desk or computer without getting sweaty and dirty by manual work so why not make an adjustment to the practice of wudu/ablution? Wudu traditionally consists of washing the face, arms, wiping the head and washing the feet with water in this order before one begins the prayer. Zizinia's point that performing this ritualistic washing is rarely practical for women and its difficulty may cause delays or skipping one's prayer times definitely resonates in many believers. I would argue that if her statement is made available for a wider audience and discussed among public scholars of Islam on different platforms, it might lead to some productive debates.

Zizinia's approach to Islam is through a script-focused close reading, that is not bound by the traditions or authorities. In fact, as quoted above, the Quran is the only book which she truly loves, remembers, and is knowledgeable about by heart (Ezer 2019a, 103). Unlike Sara and Emilia, her witnessing "many misleading and violent thoughts which are spread by some people who call themselves sheikh" didn't disincline her from Islam. Her stance is similar to Sama's who told me that the Syrian youth lost faith in them when most sheiks sided with the dictator, but it didn't affect her deep belief (75). Zizinia convincingly argues that "I strongly doubt that their religion is the one that God wants us to follow" and settles in the "version of Islam that I was taught in the family" (103) and of Father Paolo's Islam (101-102). Sama, Muna, and Rawan also stated the same fact at some point during our conversations; people, youth in particular, lost their trust and respect to many religious authorities of Islam in Syria who sided with the regime after 2011.

Hiding my emotions in unfolding of Zizinia's deep-seated belief in Islam and interfaith dialogue with other Abrahamic religions was challenging as my own religio-spirituality is shaped in similar empathetic feelings. As I discussed in the section on self-reflexibility with a reference to Sprague about relational agency and transparency, I considered communicating my feelings with Zizinia as a means of reciprocal empowerment. After all, Sprague states that abstract individuation of ourselves in research makes it easy to objectify those we study, and there is a danger in attempting a distancing effect (Sprague 2005, 21-22). I asked Zizinia who Father Paolo was and what impact he had on this group of Muslim Syrian girl scouts, and by the end of her narration, I was in tears.

Father Paolo was an Italian monk who lived and worked at the historical monastery of Mar Musa/Saint Moses located north of Damascus. Zizinia remembers Paolo as the first foreigner she has ever met in Syria who spoke fluent Arabic with a "nice sounding accent" (Ezer 2019a, 101). During their visit to the area for a week-long school trip during a cold winter, Paolo taught the girls how to survive in nature. His self-sufficiency (living with no electricity, making cheese from the nearby goats) and his extensive knowledge of Islam impressed Zizinia the most as a 15 year old young individual. "He was clearly into promoting a religious dialogue between Islam and Christianity. I heard the most progressive interpretations of Islam from him, women's respectability, talents, and capacities as full individuals," Zizinia remembers. She recognizes the irony today that it was a Catholic Italian monk who told them "that Islam was the religion which valued females highly" and recounted "many stories about strong women during Muhammed's time that haven't been promoted today" (102). As a divorcee around the age when Khadija proposed the Prophet Mohammed who was working in her business, Zizinia recalls Father Paolo's words today on the tradition during the Mohammedan times regarding the etiquette of proposing to widowed or divorced women because of the value attributed to the Muslim women.

Probably merging her parents' and Father Paolo's interpretations of Islam in her critical mind and with multiple readings of the Quran, Zizinia's Islam has developed in an inclusive and interfaith manner, which she passes on her daughters today:

> I love my religion (...) I see many connections between Islam and Christianity. The main principles that I believe are that there is one God, an end to this life, and there is an afterlife. You need to serve other people in ethical and kind ways. (...) You are a servant on this earth and that you need to put all your faith in God with full submission. (...) One's focus doesn't need to be only on Islam. The full chain of God's letters to humankind composes monotheistic religions (103).

Earlier in this book, the permeability in boundaries of sacred and secular and the concept of "ambiguous sacred between religion and spirituality" in relation to transcendence are brought to attention (Day et al. 2013; Blasi et al. 2018). Scholars' efforts to close the contemporary religion-spirituality divide or the distinction between religious ideas and mystical experiences find embodiment in the life and words of Zizinia as in the other Syrian women whom I interviewed. When the question on special places where her spirituality gets the most intense was posed, she named two pre-Islamic spaces, the Church of Saint Simeon Stylites (the 5th century, Syria) and Yerebatan Cistern (Byzantine Emperor Justinian I, the 6th century, Istanbul), blurring the boundaries of sacred for a Muslim woman. All the while, she remains confident and comfortable in her faith.

I argue that these examples raise the significance of developing a novel discourse of Islam as a lived religion as opposed to the versions imposed by the so called authorities of Islam.

Parallelism between Zizinia and Dima's religio-spiritual trajectories can be drawn because of their liberal Muslim family backgrounds and their strong rootedness within Islam despite the challenging war and pre-war practices of Islam in Syria that are patriarchally interpreted. In retrospect, Dima accepts that her taking the hijab was caused by peer-pressure and pleasing others like her teacher of religion and classmates who wore the hijab. This period lasted for three years, between the ages of 15 to 18 despite her mother's protests. She took the practice to the extremes at times by keeping her scarf while sleeping or refusing to listen to the music with fears of hellfire. Today, she laughs over them and adds that she has never thought of changing her religion or deserting religions altogether.

Similar to Zizinia, Dima remembers hanging out with her Christian friends, visiting churches on special days and attending other Christian ceremonies as she was growing up. They were part of the culture and her socialization, not a soul search. Dima's journey took place inside Islam's different paths as she learned about the disparities between the sects etc. When asked about her opinion on these denominational differences in Islamic practices today, she doesn't hesitate: "Actually, according to religion, I think it's healthy practice because it's diversity," which confirms Reinhart's statement in *Lived Islam*: "Muslims themselves, or at least until very recently, have mostly been open to the notion of diverse interpretation of Islam, perhaps following the Prophetic hadith: 'in diversity there is a mercy'" (2020, 17).

The reason Dima feels at home where she has arrived today in her lived Islam can be explained by her discernment in the external (men's) interference into religion that could have been a uniting force ("maybe religions are tools to make people in the good perspective to get them united") leading to peace without erasing diversity: "What they do on the ground is not about Islam at all, it is about getting power. I try my best just to make peace with all religions, putting aside the actions of people. I always say we are all victims in that system" (interview February 16th, 2020). By separating the exploitative practices of Islam from the essence of religions in general, Dima considers all participants in the system as victims, including the ones in power. She brought up the concept of ijtihad more than once and was in favor of it.

Drawing the conclusion that all believers are victims sets Dima apart from several respondents in this book as she underlines that her personality or ideas about Islam didn't change after 2011 like most women in her circle:

> If you asked this question to other people but not me, they would say definitely yes, but in my case, no, I'm still the same after taking the decision of discarding the hijab at 18. But what's happening with some girls, after the uprising, that they had the space to explain things to themselves, away from their society, away from patriarchy, things like that.

However, Dima makes another distinction between religious performance and personality, accentuating that her wearing hijab when she went to Idlib (Syria) affected her life temporarily. "If I went there [Idlib] and didn't put on a hijab, they [locals] would give me a hard time. They won't let me in ... things like that, so such practices, they affected my life but not my personality," acknowledging that her performance takes place only "because of some people." She wore it for practicality although she no longer believes in the requirement, referring to the Quran and explains that the prophet's wives took the hijab for safety and there is no order for all Muslim women to cover their hair or head. Unlike Zizinia, who hated obeying a lifestyle that created "a conflict and hatred" in herself (105), Dima's putting headscarf was a performative act.

In addition to Lutfia, three more women, Sama, Bidaa and Muna, wore headscarves during the time of the interviews. Similar to Leila and Zizinia, they also prioritize service to people and good deeds over appearance and rote praying. Evidently, they have positive attitudes toward life and imparted many plans about the future despite the episodes of multiple displacements and separation from their families. Their expressions of strength and optimism activated my initial bias that believers might be better equipped to overcome trauma and develop a keener awareness of personal strengths (Acquaye et al. 2018; Knott 2016; López et al. 2015; Mayer 2007). The individualized forms of religiosity enable women to develop effective tactics to face the challenges of forced migration and the requirements to integrate. Another reason for my partiality stems from the accounts of Sara, Ola, and Emilia whose backgrounds radically differ from each other but they experienced several incidents of despair and depression which recurred over the years.

Facing Inexpressibility: Spirituality and Sacredness for the Non-Believers via Lived Islam

Sara, Ola, and Emilia are self-declared agnostics-atheists; and they used these two terms interchangeably during the interviews. Among the small and randomly selected pool of respondents, they are the ones who felt the need or were asked to see a therapist as a result of what they have been through before and after multiple displacements. The following section presents selected examples from their interviews to formulate a new awareness of how sacred-secular binaries' boundaries become permeable and can challenge an individual's own perceptions. In fact, I confess toying with the idea of introducing them to the concept of lived religion which might modify their insights into religion-as-lived, particularly because they reside outside of the Islam that they disliked and rejected in Syria.

In a recent book, Fedele and Knibbe acknowledge that the "religious/spirituality dichotomy is important for contemporary people and should be taken seriously" (2020, 1). I join their proposal to study what people mean when they use the word spiritual but not religious with the hopes of tackling "this dichotomy as a cultural phenomenon" (1). The selected accounts of Sara and Emilia also attest to the importance of the researcher's deep listening and submitting to their views while simultaneously connecting myself with the arguments that complicate and dismantle dualistic approaches in academia.

In addition to what she survived as a single woman in Athens after six months in Istanbul, Sara is constantly exposed to narratives of hardship and trauma due to her current job at an international NGO. She has suffered from chronic insomnia even before the war and was diagnosed with PTSD in Greece which she chose to treat with marijuana. The quotation below displays some of Sara's coping mechanisms to sustain her strength, all of which are free of religio-spirituality.

> I've got my own ways of dealing with the pain that hangs on from work. I guess everybody does as a survival tactic. I take long showers, cook, and clean the house (…) I realized that when I am cleaning the house, I can be all by myself. (…) Recently, I read an online article "12 Rules of Taking Care of Yourself," and you can also check

it out and pick the ones that work for you. (Ezer 2019a,141)

Unlike Lutfia, Sama, and Bidaa, who asked for examples and further explanations of spirituality, Sara's comments demonstrate a well-thought-out stance regarding the term and create room for both self-fashioning and redefining religio-spirituality:

Well, as you know, I am an atheist, or rather an agnostic, but this doesn't mean that I am not spiritual. I disconnect this wonderful word from religion. Anyone who triggers special emotions in me, empowers me by guidance and wisdom, or makes me a better person contributes to my spirituality and is a spiritual person. Spirituality relates to inexplicable feelings. (144)

Despite Sara's choice to appreciate a self-defined spirituality which is devoid of God, her words remain an epithet of lived religion based on the literature that I reviewed for this study. As "the embodied and enacted forms of spirituality that occur in everyday life," her examples lead me again to the works of Ammerman, Pargament, Orsi, and Soelle (Ammerman 2014, 189).

Temporally, Sara's religio-spiritual transformation coincided with Emilia's, but unlike Emilia whose spirituality is also free of God (as will be mentioned in detail following Ola's story below), there was an enigmatic person behind it:

When I was 15, I had a teacher who changed my life. Let's call him "Mr. Spiritual." He was a patient and charismatic man who took the time to introduce me to some new ideas and worlds through books and conversations. During this period, I began to question Islam and religion in general. I realized that I was a unique individual and nobody had the right to impose their lifestyle or to prevent me from seeing the real me inside. Before I met him, I pretty much lived in a small, dark box without much knowledge about the rest of the world. Once my mind expanded with new and fascinating ideas, I denounced religion and stopped practicing. I would call myself agnostic today but things may change in time. (Ezer 2019a, 133)

The tradition of religion that Sara was brought up in must have negated the uniqueness of individuals, which in turn led Sara to blame religions in general. She interpreted them as stumbling blocks on the path to "see the real [her] inside." Blissfully unaware of the continuing academic debates (which I become a part of) on reconceptualizing and/or merging the two concepts, Sara disconnects spirituality from her abandoned religion and only by doing so she can embrace it fully. That she gave considerable thought to this concept was clear in her willingness and clarity when I asked her the related questions. Unlike Lutfia or Leila whose brevities on the topic were telling for very different reasons, Sara had a lot to say, especially after making connections to certain people's presences, strength, and energies:

> Spirituality can be connected to one's inner strength as well. Some people have a calm confidence radiating from them. They know what they want in life, and they are well aware of their abilities and also limitations. There is no confusion in their minds or in their ideas when they talk. Those people are admirable and I hope to become one of them some day. (145)

Although I know what Sara means via the descriptions that she provided, the idea of turning the statement "there is no confusion in their minds or in their ideas when they talk" against her proud agnosticism sounded appealing. However, I refrained. It could have been either potentially fruitful or simply rude and silencing. After all, I was following her second mentor's advice, her high school teacher whom I liked immediately based on what Sara told: "He valued listening over talking, reminding me many times, 'Sara, you need to listen more than talk. If you want to grow up, you need to listen to people, and be very careful with your words. Once they are out, you cannot take them back'" (134).

Does Sara want to become a spiritual person one day or only someone with a clear mind? In Sara's vocabulary, are all people who exude calmness as a result of knowing themselves spiritual regardless of how dictionaries define the word "spiritual"? Which cultural and historical dynamics are behind her sharp divide between religion and spirituality, and what are/will be the consequences for her?

In another instance as we were talking about work and career, Sara mentioned her manager who told one of Sara's colleagues, "I found a piece of God when I worked with Sara," before she left her position in Athens, and Sara thinks of it as "something so powerful that I'll never forget" (138). That being "praised" as a part of a non-being (for Sara) can move her so profoundly is intriguing. Besides, Sara mentioned this sentence not in the part where I ask questions about religio-spirituality but about her work life.

Analyzed through lived religion, Sara as well as Ola helped me develop a novel awareness of how boundaries of sacred and secular may become permeable and challenge an individual's own perceptions. In fact, a reconsideration of religion or an introduction to the concept of lived religion might radically modify their insights into religion, especially that they currently live outside of the Islam that they disliked and rejected in their past Syrian context.

Ola's attitude about Islam and God may seem doubly confusing for anyone who seeks to disentangle the complexities in expressions of faith or the lack of it. To balance the number of women who grew up Muslim but chose to part ways with Islam, I include segments of Ola's story here whom I met in Vancouver in Summer 2018. Unfolding of her life story as a newcomer began with her childhood which was marked by the loss of her mother from a brain tumor when Ola was seven years old. She insisted that she had no recollections of any events or people before the age of seven except the photo albums of her parents who went on regular holidays abroad which triggered Ola's imagination.

Ola is the only sibling out of six girls who failed to attend university and instead ended up in an early marriage with the hopes of liberation from her conservative elder sisters' monitoring. She adored her father who was a communist and atheist, handing her classics such as Maxim Gorky's *Mother* even when Ola was too young to grasp. On the other hand, she was sent to a Catholic school where she was trained by the nuns from France and Lebanon. She only conferred briefly that Sunday was their off day unlike the rest of Syria (Friday) and her classmates came from various different religious backgrounds. I suspect that Ola's strong prejudices against religions in general might have blocked some of the impact of her schooling that could have presented material for the context of lived religion. Yet, during our second interview she already -almost proudly- revealed some supernatural occurrences that she experienced in Syria, referring to her family members as witnesses.

In his outlining of abundant events, Orsi identifies that an abundant event presents itself as ***sui generis*** that people experience them as singular, that is, "even if they are recognizable within cultural convention -for instance, even if a culture prepares us for an encounter with witches, when the encounter happens, it is considered out of the ordinary" (Orsi 2007, 43). Ola's encounter with Khidr necessitates to be considered exactly in this context.

Khidr/Khizr is believed to be a righteous servant of God and aids those in distress. The green color associated with Khidr is also the spiritual color of Islam. Some say Khidr is the Muslim version of Elijah and referred to as the eternal wanderer, a mysterious prophet-guide and so on. One finds a variety of names, titles, and anecdotes associated with Khidr in Islamic folk literature. Both Turkish and Syrian cultures prepare people for an encounter with Khdir, not unlike the witches that Orsi referred to in his context.

Ola caught me off guard when she told me that she saw Khidr one night while she was sitting at the front seat of a car in motion in Aleppo. Ola's description of this male figure with minute details on that night is an example to what Orsi refers to as "abundant events" (2007, 42).

Khidr's presence is shared almost casually in the midst of her atheism and "modernism" (her own term as she provided plenty of examples from the educated and "modern" women of the previous generation in her family). With Ola's assertion on its/his truth, Khidr's existence suddenly became greater than the sum of her intentions, the persona she proceeds to construct for my work, her hopes and fears among other things. Khidr cannot be accounted for with reference to her beliefs but only to socio-religious circumstances. However, unlike Emilia, Ola did not resort to the terminologies of hard or soft sciences. Instead, she insisted that Khidr appeared to her on that night with his green coat and staff as he is usually described. In fact, I suspect that it was my insider-outsider status, and the assumed shared knowledge that made her even bring up the incident in the first place.

Seeing my expression, Ola added that her intuitions and visions shocked her former partner and family members several times, after adding that she occasionally has some prophetic dreams that she shared with them in the past. These events are out of the ordinary and real to those who experience them according to Orsi. People (in this case, Ola) absolutely know them not to be hallucinations, delusions, or other kinds of sensory error. The events arise and exist among people; yet, as an atheist, Ola is indecisive about what to make of them, referring to them as real and inexplicable (2007, 42-43).

Lived religion can be experienced in a secular setting as something traditional, lifelong, and part of childhood socialization (Kupari 2020). Grown up in the pluralistic religious field, Ola can be thought of enmeshed in the relationships among people, places, and histories in which the supernatural (e.g., Khidr) are embodied to such an extent that they cannot be shaken off by self-declarations of atheism or agnosticism. Emilia and Sara's responses to spirituality and transcendence attest to it as well. In fact, abundant events can be a shared notion between believers (Leila) and non-believers (Ola) of Syria even if they are reluctant to recognize them.

Describing herself as "not that 'Muslim-Muslim'" Leila thinks of "a real Muslim" as someone who is "always close to God, not only when she needs," and she accepts praying "more in difficult times and before the exams." However, she too is granted with occasional "special and inexplicable moments" (Ezer 2019a, 125). That she doesn't really feel comfortable sharing them is the reason for brevity of the section about her. The incident draws affinities to Ola's intuition about a death in her ex-husband's family when she received a call from him to which she responded

"Who died?" before he delivered her the news.

As Leila was praying one of her irregular *salats*, suddenly, she began to cry: "I used to see or hear people crying while praying, but it never happened to me before that day," she says. "As soon as I was done praying, my aunt's husband came home and announced that my father had a heart attack. It was a strange moment" (125). This abundant event aside, Leila's religio-spirituality can be set in the middle of the spectrum of the Syrian respondents. Her blending prayers/*salats* with clubbing, attending the Pride Istanbul, visibly supporting the LGBTQ community, and having non-Muslim boyfriends are reflective of the richness about the Syrian and/or refugee Muslim women at large that needs to be made more visible in the Global North.

Ola's resilience is attained not by praying to God but through a struggle against her therapists and prescriptions. She intends to be completely medicine-free and has been forming her spirituality via energy-healings. As many times as she repeated her denial of God, she referred to the power and effects of energies: "Inside me, I've positive energy, my aura. If you take my energy, I fall down. My emotional and physical being will get sick. After I left my ex, it took me almost five months to recover because he was very negative. He took my energy" (interview July 26th, 2018). I claim that Ola's spirituality has been in transition since her multiple-displacements began. She is settled in Vancouver, reunited with her two children who arrived from Dubai in 2019. Ola's faith journey is likely to go through more and major amendments in time since she too is now outside of the Islam that she rejected in Syria like Sara. Mediation of anecdotes regarding Khidr and her atheism can be best analyzed in the context of lived religion without hinting pathologies if reported by the experts of psychology or neuroscience.

Emilia, also settled in Canada (Toronto), began working after graduating university in 2018. Constructing her spirituality devoid of God, she nevertheless enjoys debates on Islam and religions in general. She saw several therapists after surviving sexual assault and multiple displacements. She takes good care of her health, and has been completely substance-free upon a conscious decision taken very early in life.[7] Her resilience emerges in the form of skepticism, challenging every context she finds herself in, and religion is no exception:

> I was raised to believe in God as a Muslim child, so I developed a
> very intimate relationship with this untouchable and invisible being
> in my own way. I believed in a kind and compassionate God, so I

[7] Lubna interview, recorded on 31 March 2021 (All the explanations on her tattoos were shared separately upon my request).

had many imaginary conversations (…) I've never really believed in monotheism but only realized it when I started questioning the entire idea in 2010. (Ezer 2019a, 88)

From my perspective, Emilia's stance in life, as the subtitle of her life story indicates, "I change every moment and am fine with it" (79), affects her not holding on to one particular belief. Because she failed to resolve "the tension or contradiction between free will of the individual and total submission to God," she eventually "denounced all monotheistic religions, not just

Islam" (89), especially after encountering Epicureanism. She believes that her "inner strength comes from [her] DNA and brain," not from God so "denouncing Islam was liberating" (90).

However, Emilia too reveals moments that can be analyzed within the context of "abundant events," something she prefers to explain in scientific terms such as "neuroscience perspective" (89). She was raised as a Muslim child by a practicing mother, and as a result, Emilia concludes: "I developed a very intimate relationship with this untouchable and invisible being in *my own way* (88, my emphasis). The god that she constructed is similar to a Sufi approach: "I believed in a kind and compassionate God so I had many imaginary conversations." The same god encouraged her to "go into [my] adventures and believe in [my] values" which gradually brought Emilia to take the decision to "let go of the identification as a Muslim" because "the God I believe in was nowhere near the one most Muslims believed in" (88). Emilia kept having dreams about supernatural beings and can still remember them vividly, particularly the feelings of transcendence that these "dreams or visions" raised in her, bringing about "a state where I was so at peace with myself that nothing on earth could affect me" (89).

Emilia's willingness to share her ideas and experiences with religion and spirituality stands out among the other women interviewed for this book although she makes a constant effort to keep her stance as an atheist. Her mind has been preoccupied with religio-spiritual issues and questions "for years." On the one hand, she declares "I've always felt the presence of a spiritual guide in me," yet her juxtaposition of "the atrocities committed by extremists of any religion, but particularly of Islam" poses a continuous challenge to embracing the abundant events or any supernatural presence (89).

Emilia's predicament reminds me of the complex problem that Orsi presents: How do scholars of religion account for experiences that are simultaneously irrational and real? Orsi has argued that events with "supernatural" characteristics are often mistreated, reduced, misrepresented, and fell victim to the problem of "reductionism" (Taysom 2012, 5). In her efforts to avoid interpretation in any religio-spiritual terms to explain her supernatural experiences or feelings, Emilia uses psychological, scientific or sociological terms, and thus reduces them to something other than what they are.

These three women suffered from physical and psychological problems due to displacement and other issues, and were assigned therapy and prescribed medicine. Yet, they were able to express themselves elegantly and transparently during the time we spent together. They commented on personal relationships, new plans about the future, an increasing personal strength and appreciation for life regardless of their (lack of) faith commitments or practices (Tedeschi and Calhoun 1995; Tedeschi et al. 2017). Although I tend to present their accounts as evidence for post traumatic growth (PTG) in this book, some months after the interviews, I received a few messages from Sara that she was feeling suicidal and depressed. Ola also expressed anger management problems, which affected her relation with her daughter and boyfriend at the time.

The respondents with deep connections to God, even in Lutfia's abusive case, shared no such or similar feelings. That this comparison continues to be an observation among a small number of respondents and should not lead to broad conclusions is worth repeating.

The reasons for these differences are definitely more complicated but the links among resilience, PTG, and faith remain to be explored as a potential theme on a broader scale in the Syrian refugees context. "Work as worship" in Islam can become part of resilience narratives too. In contrast to Lutfia's increasing religiosity, Sama thinks that she was more religious in Syria and wishes that she "could invest more time in Islam" in Germany, her new country of residence (Ezer 2019a, 69). She is careful not to miss her daily prayers and prefers practicing in solitude. Even so, she is sometimes afraid "to lose [my] faith all of a sudden. I seek refuge in God" (75). Despite her concerns, she can justify her inability to devote more time to prayers by praising hard-work and labor to improve oneself. One needs to cope with many demands in a new and unfamiliar country, such as learning different skills and acquiring a new language: "Learning German is my top priority. All these adaptation and survival efforts are distractions from my religion." However, she also "know[s] that Islam demands its followers to work hard" (74) and is convinced that using one's time efficiently and developing new skills are part of being a good Muslim.

Among other elements, Sama bases her resilience on a hadith in which the Prophet Mohammed praised strong believers "because they are more active and energetic in performing ritual prayers and noble deeds in life, whether obligatory or not" (75). Although I found the phrase "strong believer" too general, I avoided interrupting her at the time. Several months later, after completing the interview with Bidaa in Athens, I noticed similarities in her emphasis on strength as a believer. Bidaa provided several examples of the positive outcomes of her calm but determined stance in facing injustice as a believer of God. In the following, she summarizes their asylum seeking interview with her younger sister:

> The interview for family reunification was stressful. We were told that only one sister would be sent to Germany since we were both over 18 years old, and the other would receive asylum in Greece. As soon as my sister heard the news, she began to cry so I told her to calm down and pray. I was very relieved that they chose her for Germany and not me. (151)

Bidaa believes that praying grants a person strength and resilience, and forms an inseparable and inevitable link between them. She practices it at all times including when the risk of attack was an issue on her way to performing ablutions before the morning prayer at the refugee camp in Moria on Lesbos Island (150). The mode that Bidaa narrated her journey from the beginning (to Turkey and Greece) reads as a series of miracles granted by Allah (147-161). She managed to sustain herself active and energetic throughout as exemplified in the following statement: "It was not too difficult to find a house since God has been with us and heard our prayers all along" (151). Bidaa confidently qualifies for what Sama previously referred to as a "strong believer" (75) while expressing her wish to become more stalwart: "I have always been a strong person, especially when I witness injustice, I get even stronger while demanding justice. It's my nature" (158). In fact, she stands out among the respondents as one of the most self-confident women and the embodiment of PTG with her appreciation for life, joyfully enlarging her network in Athens, and making new plans for the future.

Somewhat closer to Leila in her approach to religion on the spectrum, Muzna Dureid was raised by the practicing Muslim parents whom she adores and lives with (2021). She is a strong-willed, hardworking activist whose struggle in gender equality informs her work with refugees and otherwise. Similar to Zizinia's accounts of growing up, Muzna too was "okay with the way Islam was practiced in" her circle until 2011 when she witnessed how the regime was "using religion to exploit and control people like sheep" during the war (Ezer 2019a, 61). She evaluates that "this whole thing affected my practice of Islam negatively and I stopped in 2014. (…) The role of religion in our society and politics after the Revolution affected me a lot. I cannot practice religion when I know that human morality should be demonstrated by our behavior, not by religion" (61). It is worth noting that Muzna's repulsion and rejection of Islam is bound in a specifically post-2011 Syrian context so it is likely to change over time.

The selected quotations above demonstrated the diversity in interpretations of Islam among Syrian women with a focus on the use of the Quranic verses, resilience and PTG, and practicing "work as a service to Allah" in the context of adaptation and survival in times of struggle. Coping with trauma involves processing loss(es) and rebuilding of one's worldviews of self and others, expressiveness, and empathy. However, these positive changes are not necessarily related to or triggered by faith commitments or submission to God. The interviews revealed that having been forced to clarify life's meaning, one's priorities, and ethics can indeed be very closely related to one's religion but not always. The respondents' life accounts can be analyzed in the concept of lived religion through modified or discarded practices during and/or after the displacement.

Islam 101: Inquiries on Hijab, Informing Missionaries, and Perceptions of Refugees

In an earlier section on representations in this book, a preconceived concern of judgment by the members of the host community is mentioned, and how it might affect the self-image of the newcomers, causing discontent and awkward moments at times (Harandi 2019; Beaman, Selby, and Barras 2017). What I find more troubling is the fact that most refugees have to deal with more pressing non-religious concerns in their new environment and are not necessarily prepared for the questions around presumed religious identity. Bidaa stands out among the self-identified Muslims whom I interviewed with her strong frame of mind:

> There are many other issues [aside from her hijab] that I am constantly interrogated about by non-Muslims; abstaining from pork, alcohol, and premarital sex are among the most popular ones so far. My strongest reference person has been Zakir Neik, a Muslim scholar of comparative religions. His talks and lectures can be found on Twitter and YouTube. We are like messengers here in Europe. People hear a lot of bad things about Muslims. I keep telling them "Read, read, read…. Don't remain ignorant." For the ears which are genuinely ready to listen to us, we need to be prepared. (Ezer 2019a, 156)

Bidaa is an exceptional advocate compared to many Muslim women who become indifferent and quiet in the face of ignorance and inappropriateness of the questions in their host countries. Some others are annoyed by them and even turn down invitations to socialization events in mixed groups (Harandi 2019, 34). After years of living abroad, I admit sometimes I approach the verge of asociality as well, especially at post-conference and/or welcome receptions that one is expected to attend. Meeting Bidaa proved to be refreshing in this sense.

Bidaa mentioned that several Christian women missionaries approached them upon their arrival to Greece. She kept quiet for their first few visits but then her patience was exhausted:

> I couldn't hold my tongue and told one of them that I knew Jesus better than she did. I began to quote lines from the Quran where the Son of Mary was mentioned and implied that my knowledge of her prophet is more recent and reliable than the contested man-made versions that she held in her hands. (...) When you think about it, most Christians across the world have been following not Jesus' but our Prophet Mohammed's lifestyle: They get married, raise families, and engage in worldly matters as much as the spiritual realm and practices. They don't turn the other cheek when someone treats them unfairly, do they? They go to the court and seek retribution, which is sharia. (Ezer 2019a, 157)

After the conversation and making use of her oratory skills acquired in law school, missionaries left the family alone. Bidaa also had many episodes with strangers to share with me on why she wears a hijab and why women in general would choose to wear one. I feel embarrassed on behalf of these host country citizens that they can ask this question especially when they are not befriended with the women in headcovers. Bidaa playfully comments on another common question after we decide to drop the worn-out and politicized subject of hijab and move on:

> Explaining the ban on drinking in Islam is easy since the negative effects of alcohol on mind and body are very clear. It doesn't take a genius to see why a religion would ask its followers to avoid alcohol or drugs. Islam completes the previous religions so it is a reminder of the old religions' uncorrupted states. Monotheistic religions are like a tall building and Islam is the end floor of this building. (157)

The representational issues regarding a Syrian woman refugee outside of Syria are not bound to the Global North, and not always addressed as enthusiastically, patiently or defensively as Bidaa does. Dima, who has been living in Turkey and speaks fluent Turkish, displayed fluctuating responses during our interviews when it came to non-Syrians' opinions on how Syrian refugee women should look or behave. In 2019, Dima represented Syria in the Young Change Makers program which took place at the Università della Svizzera Italiana, a public Swiss university. It was an international gathering of young people, and the questions of a male participant particularly stuck with Dima:

> I was meeting people from all around the world, the Middle East, and everywhere. The moment they [the participants] started to know me, like "She's Syrian, oh my God, what is she doing here?" [laughter] He asked me "Why are you here, how did you come here?" I was like "What do you mean?" He said "You are not like a refugee. How do you travel without someone accompanying you?" I think he was from France. I smiled. (…) He later told me "I thought you'd shout at me," I said "No, you guys have the best perfume in the world so I can't." He was like "What? Are you for real?"

Dima's coping and communication strategies differ from Bidaa's. She doesn't enjoy being pigeonholed in a defender's position and is exhausted by the lack of control regarding her environment. Meetings in Turkey where the main agenda is refugees and when she is the only Syrian among the attendees are particularly challenging.

> I don't have to defend myself. I tell you my experience but I don't want to prove that I'm right. I just explain in simple terms, if you like it, fine, if you didn't, okay. I don't take the defensive. Maybe in 7-8 years, I have become this person I'm today. Because it's hard sometimes that you're in a meeting and they speak badly about refugees, they don't consider you as Syrian or as a refugee, they start to speak in front of me about them. What should I do? How much control do I have in that situation, how to deal with this kind of problem?

One wonders which is more disappointing for Dima: Ignorant questions posed by the educated and supposedly open-minded youth at an international gathering or by a man on the street, like a taxi driver in Turkey who is not even aware of the faux pas or the stereotypes that embark as soon as a daily encounter takes place:

> I don't consider it a bad way but it makes me a little bit sad. When I take a taxi, from my Turkish, the driver knows that I'm not Turkish so he asks where are you from? I say: "Suriyeliyim [I am Syrian]." He is like: "No, you don't look like Syrian." I ask him: "How should we

look?" I mean… They say you don't look poor and refugee-like. I really don't like to hear but they say it because they feel comfortable talking with me. Then, I try to explain that where we lived nicely, it's because of the war that most refugees are now poor. You know many of them used to be millionaires, it is about being human.

Dima's fair skin and Caucasian features would allow her pass as any "white" European since she doesn't wear a headscarf unlike Bidaa. Smith's argument (mentioned earlier) that direct narratives of women refugees serve to disrupt dominant narratives and support producing a counter narrative is at work in these sections, embodied in the words of Dima and Bidaa as in others. The people of the host countries regardless of their background and education seem to fail in "more nuanced understandings of displaced women's agency" and keep reflecting the "dehistoricized representations of victimized refugee women" on the Syrians whom they encounter in daily life (2018, 57). I chose to juxtapose Dima's attitude with Bidaa's as her construction of a victim ("I always say we are all victims in that system") radically differs from the people Dima has to deal with. Under no circumstances, Bidaa accepted or performed a victim's role, and always raised her voice in the presence of authorities. Her deep submission to one and only Authority, and that nobody but God is going to help her maintain her agency and keep it steady and resilient.

(Im)Permanence, Tattooing Female Body, and Its (In)Significance in Lived Islam

Lubna was an activist, living and working in Gaziantep at the time we met in 2020. She is married to a Syrian man with whom she cohabited before marriage, and they have a son who was born in Turkey. Enriched with her more than two dozen tattoos, Lubna's religio-spiritual practices and background knowledge in Islam are evidence for varied interpretations of Islam as lived.

As the daughter of secular Muslim parents, Lubna remembers reading the Old Testament, the New Testament, and the Quran at an early stage in life. After her basic questions about religion (such as "What's the benefit of God's burning people in hell forever?") fell on deaf ears and resulted in her dismissal from the class when she was around 11-12 years old, she assigned herself some homework. Reading books about different sects and denominations such as Shia, Ismailis, and Druzes was included in her efforts of a self-religio-spiritual development, especially after she realized how "critical thinking" was missing in the daily discourse in Syria. She observed that some traditions took hold of Islam and claimed truth. In 2008, Lubna "felt free from all these faith groups and continued [her] spirituality without any attachments."

However, our interview made it clear that she continues asking questions and occasionally finds herself in challenging positions such as responding to her son's questions on God and Islam. She asks me rhetorically at the interview: "Why don't we discuss both daily and existentialist questions together since in the Quran, there is of course the sharia sections, and even sex is discussed?" I deem it a valid question indeed, considering the immersive structure of the Quran and the range of topics covered in it. Non-theological Quranic readings (such as Carl Ernst's) which explain both the daily and the existentialist within a historical context and from literary perspectives can serve to curious and critical minds like Lubna's (Ernst 2011). Lubna underlines that it is important to differentiate between tradition and religion, and "There is nothing in Islam against women's public involvement. Most sheiks are intentionally strengthening the traditional Islam because it is easier to control people in this way" (February 17th, 2020).

Lubna doesn't wear a hijab, which, she says, allows her to pass as a regular migrant woman in Europe or in Turkey. However, she acknowledges discrimination against hijabi women in Europe and in certain circles of Turkey. Lubna adds that the most common facial and verbal responses that she receives are either of surprise or shock, especially if her tattoos are visible.

What makes an individual to reject, rebel or intensify one's religio-spirituality in the face of traumatic occurrences is an intriguing question, which came up during most interviews. Notably after surviving the siege of Ghouta, chemical weapons attack, and becoming a witness to massive violence and atrocities, Lubna, a non-practicing Muslim until then, began praying and fasting "in order not to go insane." Many women have had fluctuating decisions and practices on how to live one's faith, and they witnessed their friends and family members' going through similar if not more radical periods as they did. Lubna's husband, for instance, was among the "many [who] stopped practicing and felt anger toward God for what was happening in Syria" (February 17th, 2020). Her soul leaned in the other direction.

After Lubna and her husband arrived in Turkey and settled in a relatively safer life and fulltime jobs, her faith practices gradually faded away with the exception of Ramadan. Fasting has always been a steady ritual for her. She recalls one particular incident where she explicitly links the patriarchal dominance to intervention to her lived religion, and how she defended her stance in a public encounter with a Syrian man:

> We were out eating and drinking in this restaurant, and the next day was the beginning of Ramadan. I practice fasting, and it is not related to my changing ideas before or after the Revolution. So I asked the waiter to bring me some food for *sahur*[8], but this man began to comment that I shouldn't be drinking if I'm going to fast the next day. He even said, "You should stop 40 days before Ramadan," which has no foundation in religion. I told him that the hadith he refers to doesn't belong to the ones that we consider *sahih*, that is, more reliable or authentic than some others. He was shocked that I have this knowledge and can discuss it with him. This is the thing with most Arab men that they see the right to correct you just because you are a Muslim woman. He wouldn't criticize a man like this (February 17th, 2020).[9]

Because I valued and was quite surprised by this account, I shared it anonymously with some of my relatives and friends who told me in return at least 2-3 similar anecdotes from their own circles. There was always this uncle or that in-law who would be drinking his *rakı* every night with an assortment of mezes except the month of Ramadan during which he fasted and prayed.[10] The first evening of Eid, he would resume his daily intake of alcohol as if he wasn't the one who had the willpower not to drink for a full month. One can encounter several similar examples of temporarily withdrawals from various acts of worldly matters which dismantle the pious or practicing Muslim image as it is often depicted in the Global North. In fact, Schielke and Debevec's edited book *Ordinary Lives and Grand Schemes* (2012) include several comparable examples across the Islamic world, ranging from Egypt to Burkina Faso. Family customs and background, different types of embedded ritualized actions in history of the regions in question enable flexibility and room for personal interpretations which can be studied under lived religion.

Dima's ideas on alcohol intake are also telling as her criterion was clear on not to do any harm if/while drinking, something she deliberately separated from Islam. Yet, her references carry elements of religion even when she argues that she is not religious so her "judgment of drinkers" (she pauses and adds "I am not sure if judgment is the right word but...") relates to "value and manners." She proceeded to explain that irrespective of "the drinking person's religious background, race, gender, and whether she wears

---

[8] Sahur/suhur is the meal consumed early in the morning by Muslims before fasting (sawm) before dawn.
[9] Selected interview passages by Lubna until here were recorded on 16 February 2020.
[10] Rakı is made of distilled grapes and anise, and considered the national alcoholic drink of Turkey.

a hijab, they shouldn't harm or hurt anyone" (June 07th, 2022). That Dima can casually associate a hijabi as a potential drinker is probably an unusual mental picture for the "Westerners" (lacking a better capturing term here) but confirms the blurry and shifting boundaries in the everyday Islam. It is complementary to the above mentioned family relatives' practices and Lubna's transition from a night of drinking to the dawn of fasting at a restaurant.

Some may argue that these examples are the exceptions of the rule or would be considered a blasphemous cocktail of religion by the majority of Muslims. I disagree. I have grown even more skeptical about this exceptionalism approach during my research as I interviewed the women from Syria whose wide range of religiosity and interpretations of Islam display different pictures. In the next section ("Where is the Survivor's Allah?" the reader will encounter an agnostic woman in hijab whose words changed my perception of any hijabi or fully veiled women for good. However, I will continue with the topic of having permanent tattoos first, which also emerged as part of this colorful picture of lived Islam.

Morello et al. (2021) explore tattoos as expressions of college women's inner lives, a venue for women to manifest their religious and spiritual experiences from a lived religion perspective. Their conclusions and some of the quotations by the respondents at an East Coast college in the U.S. are strongly in line with what I gathered from the comments of the Syrian women with tattoos whom I interviewed. In this specific context, tattoos function as part of a spritual healing process and expression of their inner quest. The physical pain of the tattoos can be interpreted as "an external manifestation of what was going on in their inner lives" (12).

Although their numbers are limited, my study demonstrates that the three women out of thirteen who happened to work full time during the time of the interviews didn't manifest any concern about their visible tattoos unlike the female American students. This creates room not only to challenge and reverse the Oriental women's image (repressed or victimized) but also juxtaposes it with the Christian American young women's representations based on the interviews on their tattoos and beliefs. One commonality between the two female groups (Syrians and U.S. college attendees) is that none mentioned any kind of conversation with a religious authority prior to going to a tattoo parlor even in the cases of clearly religious tattoos (e.g., a Catholic motto, a Buddhist sign, or Allah in Arabic) about getting tattoos. These women found enough freedom in the lived religion realm "to decide what to reveal or hide, without care for the established authorities within the religious field" of Islam or Christianity (12). The participants with tattoos "express their inner lives in their own ways, mixing religious and mundane signs" (13). Their conclusion that "tattoos are available cultural venues for women to express their spiritual, religious lives with creativity and autonomy from the expectations of their religious traditions" certainly resonates with my participants from Syria too.

The contemporary studies indicate that many Muslims have tattoos and do not consider it as a transgression of their faith although getting tattoos in Islam seems to be discouraged or disapproved (Nasir 2016; Mohammad and Sodiq 2017). Lubna, for instance, highly values her numerous permanent body decorations and attributes multiple meanings to them. The ones that stand out the most in her accounts are empowerment, recovery, freedom, and memory. As the following accounts demonstrate, not even once she mentioned tattoos' link to Islam or whether she considered it as transgression. They rather serve as mementos of places, people, and feelings that she needs and wants to remember.

Morello et al. present cases in which respondents "got their tattoos as a sign or source of stability in the midst of what they perceived to be uncertain times" confirming what Lubna and Sara in particular articulated. Lubna had Allah and *muqatila* (a female warrior) tattooed on her skin "because I thought this is something that is like… anchors to me, values, something steady in my life" (February 17th, 2020) whereas Sara's tattoo of "nothing is forever" on her arm potentially works both ways, which will be explained after Lubna's accounts of her tattoos.[11] It is worth noting that Allah's name was mentioned only in passing: "I wrote the names of the cities that mean to me, Damascus, Homs, also I wrote the name of Allah, the name of my son…" Lubna was simply listing some of the letters and symbols that were tattooed on her body from where she draws spiritual strength as they seem to function like a memory talisman and a record of overcoming an obstacle:

> When I started tattooing my body, I was getting out from a very hard and tough experience and it affected me a lot. (…) Everything I found is something that gives strength to me, like, my latest tattoo is an Arabic word that means female warrior, and I was in a very bad period also under a huge umm… pressure.

Her words in fact serve as a memory talisman, particularly in the following: "I tattooed this word female warrior which means I am not going to surrender to the bad circumstances that I am living in now." That resilience can be constructed via physical intervention to the skin in the form of multiple tattoos by Muslim women believers is a novel disclosure that is

---

[11] Lubna interview, recorded on 31 March 2021 (All the explanations on her tattoos were shared separately upon my request via whatsapp texting and voicemails).

worth investigating further by increasing the number of female respondents.

Encountering the same argument in Sara's narrative, who is a self-acclaimed spiritual agnostic, comes as no surprise. Her status as a single and younger woman than Lubna, Sara's contingent existence in Athens and her perception of temporality help her bond with the tattoo on her arm in black Arabic letters which translates as "nothing is forever" (Ezer 2019a, 139). Sara's summary of her philosophy (treating all beings gently, infinite capacity of human beings, and reminding oneself of ephemerality) resonates with Sufism but I am cognizant that it is due to my own background and interpretation of faith: "The thing I pay the most attention to in life is not hurting others. When I say "hurt," I include any kind of injury, not just physical," Sara says. Then, she adds: "I believe in the immense potential of human beings, that we can realize anything we imagine. I also remind myself that everything in this world is temporary and this includes all the difficulties and problems that hit us in life. I feel better when I look at my tattoo and remember "nothing is forever" (146).

Emilia's first tattoo was Allah in Arabic, which she got in Syria as a teenager: "While I was going through many difficulties during my early teenage years, I had strong faith in God. Although I grew out of it in time, I still like to keep this tiny tattoo on my finger since it reminds me of where I was and how I ended up here" (Ezer 2019a, 92). Her secular skin decorations are floral and were attained many years later in Canada:

> I love roses and attribute different meanings to them such as Aphrodite, philosophy, and beauty. I love flowers in general: Lavender, daisies, and jasmine of course! It is hard to choose one over another. I guess rose is still my favorite. I like tattoos on people's bodies. They are about little ideas and stories. (92)

Emilia captures the point concisely by referring to the combination of ideas and narratives behind most tattoo carriers. The value and meaning attributed to them vary as in the case of Lubna's dozens of personal expressions in comparison to Emilia or Sara. They become not a symbol of but the permanence itself:

> My body is the anchor for myself, being in this world, especially for me as a refugee without home, without visible memory, without old relations (…) so if I put this on my body, this will remain with me and move with me everywhere I go, this stays with me, I am not going to leave them in Syria or any other place this time. (February 17th, 2020)

I contend that something paradoxically immanent emerges particularly in

Lubna's construction of her tattoo narratives, that is, the materiality of the tattoo as a permanent talisman as long as she is alive. She is cognizant of their religio-spiritual power because she doesn't refer to them as psychologically comforting or a placebo effect. The effect is beyond the terminology of social sciences as it crossroads with Orsi's concept of abundance. From an external viewpoint, tattoos' functionalities can be observed more effectively and less judgmentally in the light of lived religion. Lubna's tattoo accounts can help researchers to flesh out what I see as the unheard or unrecognized premises in daily Islam practiced by women.

The research by Morello et al. conclude that tattoos reflect women's inner lives, spaces of autonomy, struggle, and creativity. I agree with Morello et al. that women's tattoos can serve "to both challenge social mandates and exercise autonomy and socially regulated expressions" (2021, 14). I add to their conclusion that when the context is extended toward the geographies like the Middle Eastern or Asian countries, tattoos can also help reversing some of the stereotypes regarding the so called "Oriental" and/or Muslim women.

Where is the Survivor's Allah after a Deep Trauma?: A Process of Un/Binding

Among the thirteen respondents, Muna's experiences with the war in Syria stood out as deeply traumatic. In fact, during the process of seeking volunteers who would share their religio-spiritual experiences for my study, her name was mentioned more than once. My feeling is that her survival story was well known and respected quietly among the Syrian NGO women's circle that I communicated with. Hers was the most challenging interview that I conducted in the past six years.

Before the Revolution (2011), Muna was a practicing Muslim of her own choice since her parents never pressured their children about religion with the exception of Ramadan:

> Because fasting is something more than just not eating or drinking. It is a collectively practiced thing so we all observed it. I remained a believer until the day I witnessed eastern Ghouta chemical attack. True that I've always been a skeptical person, always asked questions about religion; but on that day, I couldn't say my prayers. I was silent, the words didn't come out during the salat.

Muna is the fourth sibling of six sisters and one brother. During the Ghouta siege, her family was hiding in the basement of an apartment building together with several other people. Men took turns to fetch drinking water that was delivered by the aid groups. When Muna's brother's knock on the basement door was delayed and Muna too heard the shotguns, which became the norm rather than abnormality, she decided to go up to the roof and check what was going on despite her parents' objections. She has always been the rebel hiding behind her conservative clothes and headscarf. "I am the professional one among you," she defended her ominous impatience referring to her degrees in Pharmacy and congestive heart failure. She found her brother severely wounded, shot in the head, bleeding profusely. "I did the CPR, I did everything I could; he died in my arms," Muna chokes, the only time when she couldn't hold her tears during several hours of the interview.

> All my clothes were soaked in blood. It was when I looked up at the sky and asked God: "Why have you forsaken us, why is this happening?" I kept asking. On that day, I became an atheist, and announced it even to my pilgrim parents who believed that they would meet their only son in the afterworld. On that day, I couldn't stand hearing the call to the prayer either. (February 18th, 2020)

The tragedy happened in August 2013, after Muna had already witnessed massive killings due to the chemical weapons attack. A staunch defender of scientific knowledge and critical thinking, who got herself into trouble for teaching Darwin's theory in 2015-16 academic year in Syria, Muna tries to explain her abrupt atheism within a scientific framework: "Looking back, I can tell that it was an irrational reaction, in time, I became an agnostic," she declares to the recording machine. She doesn't believe in the presence of a soul or an afterlife. However, the rest of the interview reveals a different and a more complicated narrative.

After the loss of their house and son, the family moved first to Idlib, then to Reyhanlı in Turkey, a town bordering Syria. Muna wanted to be left alone, which is not common or easily achievable for a single woman in the Middle East who lives with her family. In Reyhanlı, Muna had an announcement for her family:

> I wanted to travel in Turkey to find the voice in me, to mourn my brother's death who was my soulmate and closest friend. I traveled in Turkey for two months. I stayed at friends' houses or hotels. I got and still get flashbacks from Ghouta days. For example, I saw one man burning to death in front of my eyes but I couldn't move. My legs were frozen. I still don't know who brought me to where I came back to my senses. One of those things that I took as *a sign from God* that he or she was with me during that unknown time and saved me. I wanted to go to Konya but never made it yet for some reason. I

feel closer to the Sufis of Islam. Even if I don't understand Persian, it feels good to listen to their songs. I am no longer an atheist. I actually *sometimes feel the presence of God*, but I deny the institutions or established religions. (My emphasis, February 18th, 2020)

Muna's account may seem to contradict her self-proclaimed agnosticism. Her practices have been changing and she has been reclaiming her religio-spirituality gradually which was shaken deeply by a series of traumatic events, culminating with the loss of her only brother in a most tragic way. 2021 marked the eight year of the Ghouta siege and Muna's first year in the U.K. where she attended courses for her second MA (Global Health and Conflict). Regarding her headscarf, Muna told me: "I wear it because it means less problems for me here [Gaziantep] as a single woman. If I go to the UK, I'd take it off." Our zoom talk in 2022 showed that she did.

By the time we completed the interviews, Muna lived in Gaziantep and worked full time for an NGO for Syrians by Syrians. Her physical and mental health was in good standing. Her resilience is outstanding and fed by the future plans and her determination for an independent and better life. When we met in February 2020, she was preparing for IELTS in case she received acceptance from a graduate school in London. She formulated her own healing in two stages and without professional help from outside (for a short term, a psychiatrist prescribed medicine but Muna quit them soon after). During both stages, solo traveling in a new country and intensive reading period on religions and mythologies, she demanded absolute isolation:

I needed time to accept reality, my brother's death, the good side is my brain blocked it sometimes. Because I don't speak the language [Turkish], I don't interact with anyone when I travel. If you got lots of friends, it makes you not focus on your journey. To accept the past, you need to be alone.

Her family respected her decision and didn't not enter her room for six months. She only had dinners with them. Then, she applied for a job in Gaziantep and moved there by herself.

Territorializing the resilience-faith link in Muna's case needs caution since her healing process demonstrates fluctuating religio-spiritual practices. One of the questions I pose in the introduction of this book was "Does renunciation or redefining a person's faith influence her coping mechanisms and resilience during and after the resettlement, and in what ways?" has an affirmative answer for Muna. The representation that emerges from her story is of a determined skeptical woman with degrees in science who will not yield in the mandates of the society or the institutionalized religions. Nevertheless, she is keen on observing the rules of the environment in which she functions, even if it means wearing a hijab and dressing conservatively as a young single Syrian woman in Turkey. Her performativity is a survival strategy until the next and more predictable steps in life are presented to her.

As for her recent (2020) religio-spirituality practices, Muna told me that she managed to build "a special bond" with God. She prays twice a day, she passes *wudu*, the ritualistic washing, similar to Zizinia, and doesn't cover her hair while praying because she prays in the intimacy of her own place. She told me that she stopped fasting after 2013 but she thinks fasting is a healthy practice from a scientific view so she is planning to fast during Ramadan. In 2019, she tried water fasting, a modified version of the traditional fasting in Sunni Islam, which I have not heard of before but decided to follow it up by emailing two scholars of Islam. One responded as "intriguing" and the other professor also welcomed the idea and wrote me back: "Obviously we need new exegesis." I choose not to disclose their names.

The practices of one's religio-spirituality during mourning periods can be fluctuating, complex, unreliable for anyone who assumes the observer's role regardless of her expertise (therapists included). Muna has been rebuilding and using her agency on multiple levels in order to heal herself with a keen awareness, knowledge, and critical thinking. One example is her recognizing the side effects of prescribed medicine, quitting when *she* wanted, and debating with the doctors due to her educational background and personality which radiates resilience and determination. Another act of agency was her decision to solo travel in a new country as a way of self-recovery, followed by her proficiency in remodeling her life in the UK through graduate education. In the meantime, her vacillating return to Islam has been a good example of lived religion that defies most formalities (wudu) while at times contradicting some basics of Islam such as believing an afterlife and soul. I hope to keep in touch with Muna if she allows me into her journey on the religio-spiritual path over the years.

Rawan's "One God, One Love" Rule: "The Rest is All Negotiable in Islam"

Rawan and I met in Vancouver in 2018 through one of the Shoe Project's activists, the playwright Zahida Rahemtulla. We went to the Museum of Anthropology at the University of British Columbia and had our first conversation at its café after the guided tour. The following two meetings also took place in Vancouver and the last one was at her flat where she was the host. I have also known her brother, an LGBTQI+ activist in San Francisco, who accepted every offer to be filmed and interviewed, but was not necessarily willing to put me in touch with his sister despite the request of our common friend and his sponsor. That I got connected to Rawan and realized that she was already someone whom I was hoping to interview was serendipitous to say the least.

Rawan mentioned that with the exception of one brother (you guessed it right), the family members are practicing Sunni Muslims. She was a challenging person to interview, which began with an outright refusal. However, she agreed to meet me and become friends, as it turned out that she suffered from isolation and her housemate was particularly noncommunicative. In time, Rawan mellowed and began recounting her ideas and life story. Among her interest areas that she wanted to share the most was religion to an extent that she even had a secret dream of getting a graduate degree in comparative religions one day. In summary, she turned out to be a helping respondent long after I left Vancouver, she kept in touch and informed me about her life.

Rawan stopped practicing Islam around the age of 25 but it didn't happen overnight. In her own words:

> I started having doubts in my religious norms and later I no longer practiced praying [salat], but [was] still fasting with my family. Because fasting in Ramadan is a kind of habit that gathers the whole family around the dining table. I stopped fasting only after I arrived in Canada, as I am alone here so gathering around the table with others in the evening didn't apply in my case, so I didn't find a rational reason for fasting other than to practice one's capability to be more patient. (personal communication April 20th, 2021)

The detailed rules of Islam in the context of a localized sharia in Syria block or interfere the bond of love between God and the follower, Rawan decided. In fact, according to her interpretations, Mohammad himself should not be as exalted as he has been (still today) in most circles of Islam. She argues with a quotation from the Quran: "If God is closer to the believer than their jugular vein (50:16), then why do we need middle people?" (October 26th 2020)

One of the striking conclusions of the interviews is the precariousness of the five pillars of Islam. Rawan is among the respondents who underlines it although she grew up in and still considers herself part of a Sunni family:

> The belief in one God is the essential thing in the Islamic religion. This is the only thing that makes me feel loyal to this religion.(...) I summarized religion in two words: Love and one God, that is it for me in my opinion. Otherwise, there are many things that I don't like, punishment of the transgressors, for example, fornication outside of

marriage. (October 26th 2020)

Rawan is very unlikely to reject religions but reclaim them by reading, thinking, and having discussions. In fact, she told me that she shares her interpretations of Islam and Christianity online (available only in Arabic), which I think is a bold gesture:

> Religion is unconditional love and also believing in only one God, what I currently do is criticizing religions, Islam and Christianity, both. I've a YouTube channel that I use as a platform to explain my views of religion because I want to tell Muslims that religion is love and to tell Christians that God is one and not three, and this is briefly my religious perspective. (October 26th 2020)

Rawan is among the believers of Islam, who considers herself on "the journey of finding the truth," and it can be achieved by sharing knowledge and reading a lot to filter out the hearsay and traditions from what she refers to as "true" religion: "The more you read about religions the more you can discern the errors and similarities. Also you can read the symbols and their meaning in religions because all religions speak in symbolic languages, that's what I believe" (October 26th 2020). Her rejection of denomination (Sunni) is already liberating as she can "mix and match" within the framework of Sufi Islam, while still challenging some persistent narratives. One example is that she believes in the Al-Ahmadiyya (a sect originated in India) perspective that Jesus did not die on the crucifix and King Pontius Pilate plotted a scenario to save his life, which made it possible to raise a family in hiding and die of natural causes.

Born and raised as a Muslim in Syria, having access to the Internet, and now settled in Canada, Rawan resides in the exact world that Reinhart describes in *Lived Islam*: "The modern world gives Muslims many choices – among them, which Islam to embrace and how to embrace the Islam they choose. These choices, thanks to high degrees of literacy, to the internet and new media, are no longer confined by the possibilities of place of residence" (2020, 155). He lists blogs, websites, books, discussion sites, and streaming media in this virtual cosmos, all of which have served as resources for Rawan as a believer.

Rawan may stand out as a conspicuous woman in her reshaping Islam in ways that Reinhart would categorize as having peculiar, postmodern features. However, women like Leila, Muna, Lubna, and Zizinia also present unique examples across the rich religio-spiritual spectrum that "an individual's world is largely constructed by choices made – how to dress, what signifying behaviors to perform, what beliefs are chosen to constitute both the self and self-presentation" (155). Is it the consumerist understanding of society, of life itself, that shapes Modern Islam along with all other religious traditions in the twenty-first century, as Reinhart argues (155)? I have reservations about concluding this way since I see religion-on-the-move as a centuries-long phenomenon where the respondents for this study are modern-day reflections of it.

CHAPTER VII

CONCLUSION

In this book, I critiqued what I consider as the problematic approach of two academic fields (Religious Studies and RFMS) for their lack or misconstruction of Muslim women refugees by using a lived Islam approach and through selected interviews with 13 displaced women from Syria. Muslim women's interpretations and practices of Islam are missing in the realm of academic knowledge in general, policy making in particular. My research was exploratory in nature and hopefully will lead to further studies in lived religion in the context of "visible and invisible Muslims" and exceed the borders of Europe from where the only collection on the issue originated (Jeldtoft and Nielsen 2012).

Derived from my observations and analysis after interviewing Syrian refugee women (Ezer 2019a), I consider this topic primarily an urgent necessity but also a long-term project. I was captivated by the diversity of the women's religio-spiritual commitments especially after the war began and displacement took place, both of which are regarded traumatic. However, I was also bothered with (as much as the Syrian women themselves) the shallowness of the contemporary discussions about Muslim women and Islam on the media, how they have been increasingly identified as a "problem" since 2001 in the political discourse of the Global North. The debates on social or mainstream media and their consumers only exacerbated if the stigmatized Muslim was also a refugee and a woman. It is only too easy to lose sight of Muslim women's concerns in this cacophony where silence can become a watchword for survival for women, especially in marginalized communities.

When most refugee women are not understood, treated or represented as the agents of their own lives, the void in the agendas of university projects and international humanitarian services regarding the needs and practices of the women's faith during the resettlement period is hardly unexpected. Research about whether and how the everyday experiences of women refugees, their concerns, fears, and aspirations relate to their personal engagement with lived Islam is scarce. Their highly personal and sometimes (potentially) socially marginal and/or secretive practices have remained hidden, and thus been excluded from academic debates of women and Islam in Social Sciences and Religious Studies.

By presenting unmediated words of Syrian women in transition regarding their religio-spiritual opinions and practices via in-depth interviewing, this book aimed to crack the gates open to this unexplored area. It is my hope that it will appeal to scholars of sociology, anthropology, and religious studies with interests in migration, social values, perceptions and representations of Islam and women refugees, or newcomers as my preferred vocabulary signifies. What emerges in their interpretations of Islam and how they practice it are agency, inventiveness and a great vitality which may cause some controversy for the authorities of the religion and conservatives at large. Deriving knowledge from women's daily Islam entails risking polemics and is a complex process. However, their negotiations beat an acceptance-rejection binary as demonstrated throughout the book and challenge not only the patriarchal face of Islam but also the academia in the Global North.

What also developed in the religio-spiritual accounts of Syrian Muslim women to me are earnest, rational and emotional efforts that use logic and evidence to persuade readers of an authentic, complex, experiential, and performative Islam that cannot be found in the academic resources or the media, especially in the Global North. Lack of knowledge about faith-based needs and practices of refugees remains a problem for the governments, healthcare staff, NGOs, human service providers, and policy makers as much as the refugees themselves whose problems need a holistic view to be resolved. The knowledge offered in this book can be used to expand the existing critical perspectives on the role of Islam in displaced women's lives.

Hira Amin (2019) demonstrates similar results to my study in interviewees' negotiating authority with individualizing their religio-spirituality as well as fragmentations of religious authority in Islam. She argues that British Muslims who are consciously trying to practice their faith are neither following traditional religious authoritative institutions or figures unreasonably nor fully individualizing or rationalizing their faith. Rather, they are engaged in a complex process of first choosing and self-restricting themselves to selected scholars and thereafter critically involving in the scholar's verdicts. In other words, it is more about understanding and partaking in the process of authority by including their own opinions, experiences with evidence from the Quran and Hadith literature. It transcends the acceptance-rejection binary as this book also validates in a different context.

Methodological approaches to researching "religion on the move" or "religiosities of women-on-the-move" clearly remain as a work-in-progress and one that will develop through more research practices in lived religion.

Looking for religio-spirituality in unlikely places and conversation lessens the risk of missing out important data on quite complex and textured expressions of faith that are revealed by the displaced women. McDaugall's work on lived Islam is a good example by highlighting household as a place for "conceptual framework for reinterpreting practices, processes, and patterns of Islamization." She argues that lived Islam can be explored via the practices of women in households which are "usually seen as marginal spaces to Islamization" (2008, 508). My positioning can lead to critical insights from a lived religion approach and I hope it contributes to several debates on how faith and religio-spirituality make life bearable and more filling for women-on-the-move without putting forward an implicit assumption, that is, one needs to abondon one's religious practices in order to take critiques on board.

In their attempts of connecting Islam to the earlier monotheistic religions, the interviewees Bidaa and Zizinia use two metaphors for Islam which welcome continuation and relationality: the end floor and the final letter. Zizinia's inclusive and existentialist approach to God includes scripts and prophets: "One's focus doesn't need to be only on Islam [as a Muslim]. The full chain of God's letters to humankind composes monotheistic religions" (Ezer 2019a, 103). Bidaa, on the other hand, uses a more solid and less dialogical metaphor: "Monotheistic religions are like a tall building and Islam is the end floor of this building" (157). The implied might be that God is the constructor for human beings to own a place called home and the residents are neighbors who should ideally be in an amicable relationship; however, it is hardly the case in apartment buildings (I grew up in an apartment and always envied houses with gardens due to their peacefulness). As someone who has been rejoiced by long e-letters and reciprocating them, my preference for a metaphor would be God as an author (authority and author sharing the same root), prophets, followers and disciples as amanuenses, and the believers as faithful readers with an occasionally earned right or urge to respond to the Author's letters. They collaborate for a morally and physically resilient life and labor.

Due to the number of interviewees, the extent of the complexity regarding the faith-based practices and their self-interpretations on building resilience during displacement remains limited. The study provides individually-wrapped life accounts and a modest amount of information while suggesting a rich potential throughout. The stories shared in this book contradict a singular, essentialised and static presentation of Islam and its female followers. They provide access to the multiple and in-between images of the displaced, creating possibilities for connections between the women and the readers.

Regarding the effects of religious commitment on refugee trauma, I am not convinced with some of the conclusions of current studies (Acquaye et al. 2018; Simsir and Dilmac 2018), and thus call for interdisciplinary research projects and dissertations on a grander scale. The questions that are designed for gathering data on religio-spirituality practices and language in RFMS can also be utilized in other cross-disciplinary projects. For instance, scholars and graduate students in the countries where the refugee population's needs demand urgent interventions as well as long-term planning by the stakeholders (not just the government bodies) can team up to work on religio-spiritual practices and building resilience.

My question about the link between resilience and faith commitments in an Islamic context proved to be more complicated than the claim that Islam provided women refugees "a meaningful framework" which sustained them during the episodes of "exile, displacement and resettlement" (McMichael 2002, 171). The conclusion derived from my interviews is that Islam doesn't essentially or necessarily offer a meaningful basis or posttraumatic growth (PTG) to the Syrian refugee women. In fact, some of them went through major crisis regarding their faith; consequently transformed, gave up or intensified their practices of Islam even in less than five years as shown in the accounts of Zizinia, Lubna, Muzna, and Muna.

On the other hand, although some women newcomers who were raised as Muslim but renounced Islam before 2011 demonstrated resilience and strength, some residual and cultural expressions of Islam still emerged in their narratives as in the selected words of Ola, Emilia, and Sara. A few of these articulations included what Orsi refers to as "abundant events," supernatural and transcendent moments which were conveyed in the intimacies of our conversations (2007, 42). Several newcomers like Sama, Bidaa, Dima, Rawan, and Lutfia argued that their religio-spirituality is not affected by the war and was reasonably rooted in Islam even if it is still a work-in-progress. My book also contributed to an earlier study by Berger and Weiss (2003), extending their criticism of the missing link between selected immigrants in the U.S. and PTG to a small group of Syrian refugee women in four countries other than the U.S.

The necessity and the urgency of service providers' inclusion of refugee women's religio-spirituality concerns remain, and the provisions (if offered by mental health and counseling services) can capture only few glimpses of the complexities regarding women's volatile and conflicting moods, expressions, and performances of Islam. The dynamics between the actual lived life (the life history) and the meanings that the individuals attach to their lived lives (the life story) are among the issues to arise in the research, and implores further investigation. I hope this book serves as a trigger for engaged social sciences scholars including practitioners (counselors and therapists in particular) in the RFMS who will take religion seriously in the intersectionality of the displaced women's struggle.

However scholars choose to define it, religion plays a much larger role at various stages of the displacement process than many researchers have assumed. Challenging as it may be, I join the selected scholars' granting primacy to the elusive and complex nature of religion as part of ordinary life, especially when the refugee women are the subjects in question. In regard to spirituality, I took almost a reverse stance, that is, I presented spirituality's multi-faceted, embodied, and enacted forms with specific examples rather than treating it as a vague and fluid concept. Combining the two terms into one as religio-spirituality was particularly helpful. This book made it clear that the selected women's experiences of spirituality and religion are/have been more complex than the religion versus spirituality distinction allows for. Expanding beyond the strict definitions Islam or Muslims helped me locate Syrian refugee women in the framework and notion of lived religion and reflect rich faith-based realities from the individual refugees' lives.

Then, there is the Women, Gender, and Feminist Studies' lack of interest in the study of religion, which has been manifested in many ways, for instance in its absence as a theme at conferences and in feminist journals. Although this absence is now being addressed as WGFS engage with the post-secular turn in the academy, the location of feminist studies of religion within a feminist academy is far from self-evident. Therefore, reminding the reasons why WGFS should show an interest in religion, or, study religion from the perspective of gender studies scholars is relevant. According to Gemzöe and Keinänen, there are two primary reasons: First, since majority of women on this planet practice some version of religion "feminism's blindness to this fact must be seen as one more way in which Western feminism excludes perspectives important to non-Western women," which is a major concern within feminist theory. Secondly, "if religion, as feminist theory has argued, is one of the most powerful ideological tools that underpins patriarchal normative views of gender and sexuality, it should be given due critical attention" (2016, 5). The material that I presented in this book proposes a good way to start to unveil this blindness in its authenticity in the context of the non-Western women.

Throughout the process, wearing feminist lenses and developing friendships enabled me to unclog the artificiality of the researcher-researched dichotomy (similar to religion-spirituality) as well as acknowledging some invisible and muted privileges with mutual respect and honesty. The soundest proposition in bridging Feminist Studies to Religious Studies so far has been Aune's argument on studying feminist spirituality as lived religion (2015). Demonstrating the extent of women's capacity to adapt and create beyond the normative and institutionally prescribed forms of Islam, I describe the knowledge that emerged from the interviews as empowering. Thus, it acts as a bridge between Feminist Studies and Religious Studies and informs both. I also envision this study as a point of entry into more pluralistic public debates where not only Syrians' but also Muslim women refugees' struggles and voices at large are taken into full consideration. Their experiences are richer and messier, thus requiring a more innovative conceptual framework to theorize them.

As displaced individuals, refugee women/newcomers are by definition in in-between spaces, a position that many social scientists favor (Kumsa 2006; Manjikian 2011; Genova and Zontini 2020). Each of them constantly negotiates and asserts a sense of selfhood, an identity that is bound to be different from their parents' in Syria and from the wider host-country identity. While their struggle between retention and rejection of Islam as taught in Syria provides a rich site for theorizing, the fluidity of the in-between space requires an equally fluid conceptual framework to analyze the empirical material. This still remains our challenge as scholars/researchers of inter/trans disciplinary academia whose space of labor in fact is not as fluid as theirs. In this regard, this study steadily criticized dualisms and followed the footsteps of the early feminist warnings such as the one by Eaton who rebukes the spirituality versus religion dichotomy. Any neglect in deeply complex histories of religious traditions can downplay hegemonic religions as inadequate and fundamentalist, something I certainly do not want to contribute to, particularly in the case of Islam (1996, 113).

This book promotes the use of religion-on-the-move as an efficient and welcoming term, introduced by Levitt (2012), expanded by Hagan (2019) and Trinka (2019b). The Syrian women respondents fall under this large umbrella phrase which underlines that displacement heightens self-awareness by confronting the woman-on-the-move with difference and the inquiry that awaits her regarding Islam and her life narrative at large.

What is offered in the accounts of women in this study will become richer and messier (in a positive sense) when similar qualitative studies in other Muslim countries such as Indonesia, Turkmenistan, Uzbekistan, and Tajikistan are conducted and combined with this book. For instance, Muslim identity in post-Soviet Uzbekistan is not necessarily based on scriptural Islam but rather on the everyday practice of religious rituals and other sources, distinguishing post-Soviet Muslims from other Muslims who learn Islam from texts and in religious schools (Louw 2007). Other examples would be the "lenient" Muslims living in northern Cyprus (Killoran 1998; Belton and Hamid 2011; Ramadhan 2020) or Russia (Schmoller 2020) or Bosnia (Aždajić 2020) whose lived Islam would display completely different landscapes for researchers. In fact, these studies combine the concepts of lived religion, everyday nationalism, and youth's engagement with Islam in unusual manners and with vivid examples.

My book provides material from RFMS for the lived religion scholars since they take the religious self-understanding of the "ordinary" people (like the Syrian respondents) as their point of departure for conceptualization. There are also recent calls emerged in academia for immigration officials that they should be better educated on how to provide appropriate care to women who are resettled as refugees in the Global North. A study in Canada shows that newcomers' experiences are very different from Canadian-born individuals and naturalized Canadians, recognizing their uniqueness. I join in the argument that by using a lived Islam approach, Syrian women's religio-spirituality may open venues "for a greater tailoring of services" to an increasingly heterogeneous immigrant and refugee population in Canada as well. In shaping newcomers' attitudes and beliefs about mental and emotional health, this book contributes to further investigation into "the role of women's background, stories, and narratives of home life, transitions, and settlement" with its focus on religio-spiritual practices (Mahajan, Meyer, and Neiterman 2021, 15).

But why to choose women subjects in particular while investigating lived Islam? Liebelt and Werbner argue that analyzing the gendered dynamics in Muslim-majority societies requires this focus, and "we have hardly begun to understand in its [women's becoming in the hermeneutics and rhetorics of Islamic texts] wide-ranging impact," a process which they refer to as "almost revolutionary" (2018, 4). Secondly, this book implores a corrective acknowledgement about the image of the Muslim women in the Global North, and thus allocates a large section on representation analysis, agency, and literature review. It not only dismantles but also reverses some of the persisting stereotypes of refugee women.

I expect this book to trigger new debates on integrating religio-spirituality into counseling and other mobility-induced services that are available and/or needed for an efficient resettlement for the displaced women who intend to build a safer life in their new countries.

When individuals claim belonging to a religion, they refer to an allegiance in various degrees, but it does not say much about their religio-spiritual practices and beliefs or their stance toward the ever-changing reality in which we humans live. In this regard, Reinhart's distinction between the domain of ritual and the "immensely diverse" appropriation of those rituals is significant. The practices belong to this rich diversity whereas the notion of "Islam" itself belongs to "the arcane but prestigious world of Muslim religious experts" (2020, 167). He argues that "Lived Islam is the native instantiation of practices and commitments to which Muslims pledge allegiance, which orient their lives, and which for them make the transcendent into the immanent" (167). The glimpses of immanence can be traced in all the selected accounts of the Syrian newcomers in this book, which includes silences, pauses, and questions as the quotations demonstrated.

Although not named or defined what lived Islam is, unlike the title of Reinhart's remarkable book *Lived Islam* (2020), one should acknowledge the valuable criticism of Frank Peter due to his early contribution to the scarce literature on lived Islam. His wording instead of lived Islam is "individualization characteristic of Muslim religiosity," that is, an Islam where the believer decides autonomously which elements of Islam she considers to be binding or not (2006, 105).

When I first began the research on this book, encountering book or article titles where "Lived Islam" is used was a rarity unliked "lived religion." As I arrived at the completion of the book, the studies -mostly ethnographical works which build on and contribute to comparative and interdisciplinary applications- have begun burgeoning (Ahmad and Reifeld 2017, Henig 2020, Vicini 2020). Malik's book *Curating Lived Islam in the Muslim World* (2021) stands out as a collection of first-hand scholarship on Muslims in the Middle East and South Asia by selected British observers of lived Islam. Its sensitivity to gender balance is worth noting as a salient number of representative British women moved away from the colonial wives stereotype and reflected on gender and Islam in Near East and South Asia by writing about the status of women, hierarchies, historic sites and regional politics. Nevertheless, I remain cautious of their disciplinary limitations, a criticism that is posed in the Introduction. Composing work that is both respected by disciplinary authorities and pushes beyond the boundaries of one's discipline is challenging.

Finally, I feel the need to state the most obvious: The theses and the debates on lived Islam or religion at large is far from being conclusive. Rather, I present this book not only an analysis of religion-on-the move by Syrian Muslim women but also as in need of being analyzed by other scholars who can recognize the great diversity of modes in which Islam has been and continues to be expressed and lived. Then, there is the "human importance" in Studies of Religion and Spirituality that Hanegraaff poetically and succinctly draws attention to in his call for "a better, more positive and constructive story to tell, not just about the 'societal relevance' of religion, but about its human importance in a world that is dominated increasingly by such major dehumanizing factors as neoliberal globalization and new public management" or the increase of "apocalyptic fears inspired by climate change, global corporate control," or the effects of a pandemic (2020, 75). By this book, I reclaim the experiential and bottom-up dimensions of what I refer to as religio-spirituality via the lived religion approach in Islam, and advocate for critical methods with and about humans in a constantly changing and contingent material world.

BIBLIOGRAPHY

Abraham, Ruth, Lars Lien, and Ingrid Hanssen. "Coping, Resilience and Posttraumatic Growth among Eritrean Female Refugees Living in Norwegian Asylum Reception Centres: A Qualitative Study." *The International Journal of Social Psychiatry* 64 (2018): 359 – 366. http://dx.doi.org/10.1177/ 0020764018765237

Abu-Lughod, Lila. "Do Muslim Women Really Need Saving? Anthropological Reflections on Cultural Relativism and its Others." *American Anthropologist* 104.3 (2002): 783–790.

___. *Do Muslim Women Need Saving?* Cambridge: Harvard UP, 2013.

Acquaye, Hannah, Stephen A. Sivo, and Dayle Jones. "Religious Commitment's Moderating Effect on Refugee Trauma and Growth." *Counseling and Values* 63.1 (2018): 57-75.

Ahmed, Erfan Feuzia. "Globalization and Women's Leadership in the Muslim Diaspora: An Intersectional Analysis" in *Muslim Diaspora in the West: Negotiating Gender, Home and Belonging*, edited by Haideh Moghissi and Halleh Ghorashi. New York: Routledge, 2010. 23-38.

Ager, Alastair, and Joey Ager. "Challenging the Discourse on Religion, Secularism, and Displacement." In *The Refugee Crisis and Religion: Secularism, Security, and Hospitality in Question*, edited by Luca Mavelli and Erin K. Wilson. London: Rowman & Littlefield, 2017. 37-51.

Ahmad, Imtiaz, and Helmut Reifeld, eds. *Lived Islam in South Asia - Adaptation, Accommodation and Conflict*. London, New York: Routledge, 2018.

Ai, Amy, Christopher Peterson, and Bu Huang. "The Effect of Religious-Spiritual Coping on Positive Attitudes of Adult Muslim Refugees from Kosovo and Bosnia." *The International Journal for the Psychology of Religion* 13.1 (2003): 29-47.

Alessi, J. Edward, Brett Greenfield, Sarilee Kahn, and Leah Woolner. "(Ir)Reconcilable Identities: Stories of Religion and Faith for Sexual and Gender Minority Refugees Who Fled From the Middle East, North Africa, and Asia to the European Union." *Psychology of Religion and Spirituality* (2019): 1-9. https://doi.org/10.1037/rel0000281

Alfani, Roger. "Refugees, Religion, and Resilience in Sub-Saharan Africa" in *The Challenges of Refugees and Internally Displaced Persons in Africa*, edited by Sabella O. Abidde. New York: Springer, 2021. 81-95.

Ali, Abdullah Yusuf. *The Meaning of the Holy Quran*. 10th edition. Maryland: Amana, 2004.

Alvesson, Mats, Cynthia Hardy, and Bill Harley. "Reflecting on Reflexivity: Reflexive Textual Practices in Organization and Management Theory." *Journal of Management Studies* 45.3 (2008): 480-501.

Amin, Hira. "British Muslims Navigating between Individualism and Traditional Authority." *Religion* 10 (2019): 354. https://doi.org/10.3390/rel10060354

Ammerman, Nancy T. "Lived Religion as an Emerging Field: An Assessment of Its Contours and Frontiers." *Nordic Journal of Religion and Society* 29.2 (2016): 83–99.

___. "Finding Religion in Everyday Life." *Sociology of Religion* 75.2 (2014a): 189-207.

___. *Sacred Stories, Spiritual Tribes: Finding Religion in Everyday Life*. Oxford: Oxford University Press, 2014b.

___. "Spiritual but Not Religious?: Beyond Binary Choices in the Study of Religion." *Journal for the Scientific Study of Religion* 52.2 (2013): 258-78.

___, ed. *Everyday Religion: Observing Modern Religious Lives*. Oxford and New York: Oxford University Press, 2007.

Anczyk, Adam, and Halina Grzymała-Moszczyńska. "Psychology of Religion(s) and Religious Studies: Into the Future." *Religion* 50:1(2020): 24-31.

Anderson, Tim. "News Media Representations of International and Refugee Postsecondary Students." *The Journal of Higher Education* 91.1(2020): 58-83.

Andrejč, Gorazd. "Infiltrators, Imposters, or Human Beings? The Slovenian Socio-Political

Imaginary, Christianity, and the Responses to the 2015-2016 Migrant Crisis." In *Religion in the European Refugee Crisis,* edited by Ulrich Schmiedel and Graeme Smith. London: Palgrave Macmillan, 2018. 39-60.

Asaf, Yumna. "Syrian Women and the Refugee Crisis: Surviving the Conflict, Building Peace, and Taking New Gender Roles." *Social Sciences* 6.3 (2017). n/a.

Aswad, Noor Ghazal. "Fragmented Paradigms of Transculturality: Negotiating Equivocal Agency in Refugee Representations in Refugee Resettlement Organizations." In *Negotiating Identity and Transnationalism: Middle Eastern and North African* Communication *and Critical Cultural Studies,* edited by Haneen Ghabra, Fatima Zahrae Chrifi Alaoui, Shadee Abdi, and Bernadette Marie Calafell. New York, NY: Peter Lang, 2020. 31-47.

Atkinson, Robert. *The Life Story Interview.* Thousand Oaks, CA: Sage, 1994.

Aune, Kristin. "Feminist Spirituality as Lived Religion: How UK Feminists Forge Religiospiritual Lives." *Gender and Society* 29.1 (2015): 122-145.

Aždajić, Dejan. *The Shaping Shaikh: The Role of the Shaikh in Lived Islam among Sufis in Bosnia and Herzegovina.* Berlin: De Gruyter, 2020.

Barnett, Michael, and Janice Gross Stein, eds. *Sacred Aid: Faith and Humanitarianism.* Oxford: Oxford University Press, 2012.

Barry, Kathleen. "Toward a Theory of Women's Biography." In *All Sides of the Subjects: Women and Biography,* edited by Theresa Iles. New York: Teachers College Press, Columbia University, 1992. 23-35.

Batson, Daniel, Patricia Schoenrade, and W. Larry Ventis, eds. *Religion and the Individual: A Social-Psychological Perspective.* Oxford: Oxford University Press, 1993.

Beaman, Lori, Jennifer Selby, and Amélie Barras. "No Mosque, No Refugees: Some Reflections on Syrian Refugees and the Construction of Religion in Canada." In *The Refugee Crisis and Religion: Secularism, Security, and Hospitality in Question,* edited by Luca Mavelli and Erin K. Wilson. London: Rowman & Littlefield, 2017. 77-95.

Beaman, Lori G. and Peter Beyer. "Betwixt and Between: A Canadian Perspective on the Challenges of Researching the Spiritual but Not Religious." In *Social Identities: Between the Sacred and the Secular,* edited by Abby Day, Giselle Vincett, and Christopher Cotter. Farnham and Burlington, VT: Ashgate, 2013. 127-144.

Becker, Carmen. "Becoming a Refugee: Muslimness and Secularity in the Constitution of the Refugee." Paper presented at the Refugees and Religion Conference, Utrecht University, September 27-28, 2018.

Bectovic, Safet. "Studying Muslims and Constructing Islamic Identity." In *Methods and Contexts in the Study of Muslim Minorities - Visible and Invisible Muslims,* edited by Nadia Jeldtoft and Jørgen Nielsen. New York: Routledge, 2012. 11-24.

Behar, Ruth. *The Vulnerable Observer - Anthropology That Breaks Your Heart.* Boston: Beacon Press, 1996.

Belton, Brian, and Sadek Hamid, eds. *Youth Work and Islam - A Leap of Faith for Young People.* Cham: Springer, 2011.

Bendixsen, Synnøve K.N. "Can the Irregular Migrant Woman Speak?" In *Gendered Citizenship and the Politics of Representation,* edited by Hilde Danielsen, Kari Jegerstedt, Ragnhild L. Muriaas, and Brita Ytre-Arne. London: Palgrave-MacMillan, 2016.

---___. *The Religious Identity of Young Muslim Women in Berlin.* Leiden, Boston: Brill, 2013.

Bendixsen, Synnøve, and Trygve Wyller, eds. *Contested Hospitalities in a Time of Migration: Religious and Secular Counterspaces in the Nordic Region.* London, New York: Routledge, 2019.

Berger, Roni, and Tzipi Weiss. "Immigration and Posttraumatic Growth-A Missing Link." *Journal of Immigrant & Refugee Services* 1.2 (2003): 21-39.

Berger, Helen A., Evan A. Leach, and Leigh Shaffer. *Voices from the Pagan Census: A National Survey of Witches and Neo-Pagans in the United States.* Columbia, SC: University of South Carolina Press, 2003.

Berghammer, Caroline, and Katrin Fliegenschee. "Developing a Concept of Muslim Religiosity: An Analysis of Everyday Lived Religion among Female Migrants in Austria."

Journal of Contemporary Religion 29:1 (2014), 89-104.

Berry, Jan. "Writing the Self- Using the Self in Feminist Theological Research." In *Researching Female Faith - Qualitative Research Methods*, edited by Anne Philipps, Fran Porter, and Nicola Slee. New York: Routledge, 2018. 203-233.

Blasi, Anthony J., Olga Breskaya, and Giuseppe Giordan. *Ambiguous Sacred: Between Religion and Spirituality. Sociologia* 52.2 (2018): 82-88.

Bondi, Liz. "The Place of Emotions in Research: From Partitioning Emotions and Reason to the Emotional Dynamics of Research Relationships." In *Emotional Geographies*, edited by Joyce Davidson, Liz Bondi, and Mick Smith. Farnham, Surrey: Ashgate, 2005. 231-246.

Bremborg, Anna Davidsson. "Interviewing." In *The Routledge Handbook of Research Methods in the Study of Religion*, edited by Michael Stausberg and Steven Engler. London, New York: Routledge, 2011. 310-322.

Buitelaar, Marjo. "Rearticulating the Conventions of Hajj Storytelling: Second Generation Moroccan-Dutch Female Pilgrims' Multi-Voiced Narratives about the Pilgrimage to Mecca." *Religions* 11(2020): 373 doi.org/10.3390/rel11070373

Bye, Hege, H. "Intergroup Relations During the Refugee Crisis: Individual and Cultural Stereotypes and Prejudices and Their Relationship with Behavior toward Asylum Seekers." *Frontiers in Psychology* 11 (2020) doi.org/10.3389/fpsyg.2020.612267

Carrière, Jean-Marie. "The Refugee Experience as Existential Exile: Hospitality as a Spiritual and Political Response." In *The Refugee Crisis and Religion Secularism, Security and Hospitality in Question*, edited by Luca Mavelli and Erin K. Wilson. London: Rowman & Littlefield, 2017. 145-156.

Castles, Stephen, and Mark Miller. *The Age of Migration*. 5th edition. London: Palgrave-MacMillan, 2009.

Cavaliere, Paola. "Women between Religion and Spirituality: Observing Religious Experience in Everyday Japanese Life." *Religions* 10. 6 (2019): 377 https://doi.org/10.3390/rel10060377

Cesari, Jocelyne. "Muslim Minorities in Europe: The Silent Revolution." In *Modernising Islam: Religion in the Public Sphere in the Middle East and in Europe*, edited by John Esposito and François Burgat. London: Hurst, 2003: 251-269.

Chaze, Ferzana, Mary Susan Thomson, Usha George, and Sepali Guruge. "Role of Cultural Beliefs, Religion, and Spirituality in Mental Health and/or Service Utilization among Immigrants in Canada: A Scoping Review." *Canadian Journal of Community Mental Health* 34.3 (2015) https://doi.org/10.7870/cjcmh-2015-015

Dagtas, Secil. "Inhabiting Difference across Religion and Gender: Displaced Women's Experiences at Turkey's Border with Syria." *Refuge* 34.1 (2018): 50-59.

Dasti, Rabia, and Sitwat, Aisha. "Development of Multidimensional Measure of Islamic Spirituality." *Journal of Muslim Mental Health* 8.2 (2014): 47-67.

Davie, Grace. "Believing without Belonging: Is this the Future of Religion in Britain?" *Social Compass* 37.4 (1990): 455-469.

Davies, Charlotte Aull. *Reflexive Ethnography: A Guide to Researching Self and Others*. Abingdon: Routledge, 2008.

Day, Abby, Giselle Vincett, and Christopher R. Cotter, eds. "Introduction: What Lies Between: Exploring the Depths of Social Identities between the Sacred and the Secular." In *Social Identities Between the Sacred and the Secular*. Farnham and Burlington, VT: Ashgate, 2013. 1-4.

de Jager Meezenbroek, Eltika, Bert Garssen, Machteld van den Berg, Dirk van Dierendonck, Adriaan Visser and Wilmar B. Schaufeli. "Measuring Spirituality as a Universal Human Experience: A Review of Spirituality Questionnaires." *Journal of Religion and Health* 51(2012): 336–354.

Deeb, Lara. *An Enchanted Modern - Gender and Public Piety in Shi'i Lebanon*. Princeton, NJ: Princeton University Press, 2006.

Denzin, Norman. *Interpretive Biographies*. Newbury Park, CA: Sage, 1989.

Derks, Freija, and Srdjan Sremac. "Negotiating the Sacred: The Lived Religion of Eritrean Newcomers and Their Process of Integration in the Netherlands." *Practical Theology* 13.6 (2020): 594-608.

Dillon, Michelle, and Paul Wink. *In the Course of a Life Time - Tracing Religious Belief, Practice, and Change*. Berkeley: University of California Press, 2007.

Donnan, Hastings, and Martin Stokes. "Interpreting Interpretations of Islam." In *Interpreting Islam*, edited by Hastings Donnan. London: Sage, 2002.

Dückelmann, Antonia. "Refugee Representations and Discourses in Australian Newspapers during 1992-1993 and 2015-2016." MA Thesis, Radboud University, 2018. https://theses.ubn.ru.nl/handle/123456789/6377

Eghdamian, Khatereh. "Religious Identity and Experiences of Displacement: An Examination into the Discursive Representations of Syrian Refugees and Their Effects on Religious Minorities Living in Jordan." *Journal of Refugee Studies* 30.3 (2017): 447-467.

Eppsteiner, Holly Straut, and Jacqueline Hagan. "Religion as Psychological, Spiritual, and Social Support in the Migration Undertaking." In *Intersections of Religion and Migration: Issues at the Global Crossroads*, edited by Jennifer Saunders, Elena Fiddian-Qasmiyeh, and Susanna Snyder. New York: Springer, 2016. 49-70.

Erhard, Franz, and Kornelia Sammet. "Everyday Lived Islam of Young People from Muslim Migrant Families in Germany." In *Young People and the Diversity of (Non)Religious Identities in International Perspective*, edited by Elisabeth Arweck and Heather Shipley. Cham: Springer, 2019. 221-240.

Ernst, Carl. *How to Read the Quran. A New Guide, with Select Translations*. Chapel Hill: The University of North Carolina Press, 2011.

Etherington, Kim. *Becoming a Reflexive Researcher: Using Our Selves in Research*. London: Jessica Kingsley Publishers, 2004.

Ezer, Ozlem. "Drawing a Narrative Landscape with Women Refugees." In *Lives Outside the Lines: Gender and Genre in the Americas*, edited by Eva C. Kapinski and Ricia A. Chansky. London: Routledge, 2020. 116-123.

____. *Syrian Women Refugees: Personal Accounts of Transition*. Jefferson, NC: McFarland, 2019a.

____. "Bir'in ve Dil'in Hegemonyasindan Kurtulmak." In *Türkiye'de Cinsiyet Kültürleri Dicle Koğacıoğlu Kitabı*. Eds. Cenk Ozbay and Aysecan Terzioglu. Istanbul: Iletisim, 2019b. 245-65.

____. "Re-Constructing Konya Through Woolly Wanderings." *Liminalities: A Journal of Performance Studies* 13. 2 (2017a): 1-19. ISSN: 1557-2935

____. "Oral History Narratives as Becoming: Traces in Northern Cyprus." In *Stories of Becoming The Use of Storytelling in Education, Counselling and Research*, edited by Sjoerd-Jeroen Moenandar and Lynn Wood. Campus Orleon: Nijmegen, 2017b. 57-76.

____. "Women's Life Writings from a 'No Wo/Man's Land': Northern Cyprus." In *Not Ever Absent —Storytelling in Arts, Culture and Identity Formation*, edited by Sjoerd-Jeroen Moenandar and Nicole Miller. Inter-Disciplinary Press: Oxford, 2015. 37-47.

____. "'Exotic Sweden': A Nordic Quest in the Winter of 2010." *Utah Foreign Language Review* 20th Anniversary Special Edition XIX (2011): 33-54.

Fadil, Nadia. "The Anthropology of Islam in Europe: A Double Epistemological Impasse." *Annual Review of Anthropology* 48.1 (2019): 117-132.

Fadlalla, Amal Hassan. "Contested Borders of (In)humanity: Sudanese Refugees and the Mediation of Suffering and Subaltern Visibilities." *Urban Anthropology and Studies of Cultural Systems and World Economic Development* 38.1 (2009): 79-12.

Fedele, Anna, and Kim Knibbe, eds. *Gender and Power in Contemporary Spirituality*. New York: Routledge, 2012.

Fedele, Anna, and Kim E. Knibbe. *Secular Societies, Spiritual Selves? The Gendered Triangle of Religion, Spirituality and Secularity*. London, New York: Routledge, 2020.

Fiddian-Qasmiyeh, Elena, Gil Loescher, Katy Long, and Nando Sigona, eds. *The Oxford Handbook of Refugee and Forced Migration Studies*. Oxford: Oxford University Press, 2014.

Fountain, Philip, and Sin Wen Lau. "Anthropological Theologies: Engagements and Encounters." *The Australian Journal of Anthropology* 24 (2013): 227–23.

Frederiks, Martha, and Dorottya Nagy, eds. *Religion, Migration, and Identity - Methodological and Theological Explorations.* Leiden, Boston: Brill, 2015.

Frederiks, Martha. "Religion, Migration, and Identity - A Conceptual and Theoretical Exploration." In *Religion, Migration, and Identity - Methodological and Theological Explorations,* edited by Martha Frederiks and Dorottya Nagy. Leiden, Boston: Brill, 2015. 9-29.

Friedmann Marquardt, Marie, Susanna J. Snyder, and Manuel A. Vásquez. "Challenging Laws Faith-Based Engagement with Unauthorized Immigration." In *Constructing Immigrant 'Illegality': Critiques, Experiences, and Responses,* edited by Cecilia Menjívar and Daniel Kanstroom. Cambridge: Cambridge University Press, 2013. 272-297.

Gade, M. Anna. *Muslim Environmentalisms -Religious and Social Foundations.* New York: Columbia University Press, 2019.

Ganzevoort, R. Ruard. "Forks in the Road when Tracing the Sacred. Practical Theology as Hermeneutics of Lived Religion." Paper presented at the International Academy of Practical Theology, Chicago, 2009.

Ganzevoort, R. Ruard, and Srdjan Sremac, eds. *Lived Religion and Lived (In)Tolerance.* London: Palgrave, 2017.

Ganzevoort, R. Ruard, and Johan H. Roeland. "Lived Religion - The Praxis Of Practical Theology." *International Journal of Practical Theology* 18.1 (2014): 91-101.

Gatrell, Peter. *The Unsettling of Europe - How Migration Reshaped a Continent.* London: Allen Lane, 2019.

Geiger, Susan. "What is so Feminist About Women's Oral History?" *Journal of Women's History* 2.1 (1990): 169-182.

Gemzöe, Lena, Marja-Liisa Keinänen, Avril Maddrell, eds. *Contemporary Encounters in Gender and Religion European Perspectives.* London: Palgrave, 2016.

Gemzöe, Lena, and Marja-Liisa Keinänen. "Contemporary Encounters in Gender and Religion: Introduction." In *Contemporary Encounters in Gender and Religion - European Perspectives,* edited by Lena Gemzöe, Marja-Liisa Keinänen, and Avril Maddrell. London: Palgrave, 2016. 1-28.

Genova, Elena, and Elisabetta Zontini. "Liminal Lives: Navigating In-Betweenness in the Case of Bulgarian and Italian Migrants in Brexiting Britain." *Central and Eastern European Migration Review* 9.1 (2020): 47-64.

Ghorashi, Halleh. "Normalizing Power and Engaged Narrative Methodology: Refugee Women, the Forgotten Category in the Public Discourse." *Feminist Review* 129 (2021): 48–63.

___. "Bringing Polyphony One Step Further: Relational Narratives of Women from the Position of Difference." *Women's Studies International Forum* (WSIF) 43 (2014): 59–66.

___. "From Absolute Invisibility to Extreme Visibility: Emancipation Trajectory of Migrant Women in the Netherlands." *Feminist Review* 94 (2010): 75–92.

___ "Giving Silence a Chance: The Importance of Life Stories for Research on Refugees." *Journal of Refugee Studies* 21 (2008):117–133.

Gore, Ross, LeRon Shults, Phillip Wozny, Frank P.M. Dignum, and Christine Boshuijzen van Burken. "A Value Sensitive ABM of the Refugee Crisis in the Netherlands." ANSS '19: Proceedings of the Annual Simulation Symposium (2019): 1-12.

Gozdziak, Elzbieta. "Pray God and Keep Walking – Religion, Gender, Identity, and Refugee Women." In *Not Born A Refugee Woman – Contesting Identities, Rethinking Practices,* edited by Maroussia Hajdukowski-Ahmed, Nazilla Khanlou, and Helene Moussa. New York: Berghahn, 2008. 180-195.

___. "Training Refugee Mental Health Providers: Ethnography as a Bridge to Multicultural Practice." *Human Organization* 63.2 (2004): 203-210.

Gozdziak, Elzbieta, and Dianna Shandy. "Editorial Introduction: Religion and Spirituality in Forced Migration." *Journal of Refugee Studies* 15.2 (2002): 129-135.

Hagan, Jacqueline Maria. "Religion on the Move: The Place of Religion in Different Stages of the Migration Experience." In *Routledge International Handbook of Migration Studies,* edited by Steven J. Gold and Stephanie J. Nawyn. London, New York: Routledge, 2019. 282-293.

___. *Migration Miracle - Faith, Hope, and Meaning on the Undocumented Journey.* Cambridge: Harvard University Press, 2012.

Hagan, Jacqueline, and Helen Rose Ebaugh. "Calling upon the Sacred: Migrants' Use of Religion in the Migration Process." *The International Migration Review* 37.4 (2003): 1145-62.

Hanegraaff, Wouter J. "Imagining the Future Study of Religion and Spirituality." *Religion* 50.1 (2020): 72-82.

Haraway, Donna. "Situated Knowledges: The Science Question in Feminism and the Privilege of Partial Perspective." *Feminist Studies* 14.3 (1988): 575–599.

Harding, Sandra. "Rethinking Standpoint Epistemology: What is 'strong objectivity'?" In L. Alcoff and E. Potter, eds. *Feminist Epistemologies.* London: Routledge, 1993. 49–82.

Harrison, Victoria. "The Pragmatics of Defining Religion in a Multi-cultural World." *The International Journal for Philosophy of Religion* 59 (2006): 133-152.

Harvey, Graham. *Listening People, Speaking Earth: Contemporary Paganism.* London: C. Hurst & Co., 1997.

Häberlen, Joachim. "Making Friends: Volunteers and Refugees in Germany." *German Politics and Society* 34.3 (2016): 55-76.

Helmer, Christine. "Theology and the Study of Religion: A Relationship." In *The Cambridge Companion to Religious Studies,* edited by Robert Orsi. Cambridge: Cambridge University Press, 2012. 230-254.

Henig, David. *Remaking Muslim Lives: Everyday Islam in Postwar Bosnia and Herzegovina.* Urbana: University of Illinois Press, 2020.

Hill, Peter, and Ralph W. Hood, eds. *Measures of Religiosity.* Birmingham, AL: Religious Education Press, 1999.

Hoffman, Marella. *Practicing Oral History Among Refugees and Host Communities.* New York: Routledge, 2020.

Hogue, Allen David. "Healing of the Self-in-Context: Memory, Plasticity, and Spiritual Practice." In *Spiritual Transformation and Healing - Anthropological, Theological, Neuroscientific, and Clinical Perspectives,* edited by Joan D Koss-Chioino and Philip Hefner. Oxford: AltaMira, 2006. 223-238.

Hollenbach, David. "Religion and Forced Migration." In *The Oxford Handbook of Refugee and Forced Migration Studies,* edited by Elena Fiddian-Qasmiyeh, Gil Loescher, Katy Long, and Nando Sigona. Oxford: Oxford University Press, 2014. 447-459.

Hunt, Mary. *Fierce Tenderness: Toward a Feminist Theology of Friendship.* New York: Crossroad, 1991.

Jeldtoft, Nadia, and Jørgen Nielsen, eds. *Methods and Contexts in the Study of Muslim Minorities – Visible and Invisible Muslims.* New York: Routledge, 2012.

Jeldtoft, Nadia. "Lived Islam: Religious Identity with non-organized Muslim Minorities." In *Methods and Contexts in the Study of Muslim Minorities – Visible and Invisible Muslims,* edited by Nadia Jeldtoft and Jørgen Nielsen. New York: Routledge, 2012. 25-42.

Jung, Jin-Heon, and Alexander Horstmann. *Building Noah's Ark for Migrants, Refugees, and Religious Communities.* New York: Palgrave, 2015.

Kamla, Rania. "Religion-Based Resistance Strategies, Politics of Authenticity and Professional Women Accountants." *Critical Perspectives on Accounting* 59 (2019): 52-69.

Kanal, Maria, and Susan B. Rottmann. "Everyday Agency: Rethinking Refugee Women's Agency in Specific Cultural Contexts." *Frontiers in Psychology* 12:726729 (2021). doi: 10.3389/fpsyg.2021.726729

Karimi, Zamila. "Informal Sacred Spaces of Worship in the Interstices: Lived Religion." *Interiors* 1.3 (2010): 265-280.

Kaya, Ayhan. "A Tale of Two Cities: Aleppo and Istanbul." *European Review* 25.3 (2017): 365-387.

Keller, Reiner. "The Complex Discursivity of Religion." In *Making Religion: Theory and Practice in the Discursive Study of Religion*, edited by Frans Wijsen and Kockuvon Stuckrad. Leiden: Brill, 2016. 319-28.

Killoran, Moira. "Good Muslims and "Bad Muslims," "Good" Women and Feminists: Negotiating Identities in Northern Cyprus." *Ethos* 26. 2 (1998): 183-203.

Kiwan, Dina. "Syrian and Syrian Palestinian Women in Lebanon: 'Actors of Citizenship'?" In *Empowering Women after the Arab Spring*, edited by Marwa Shalaby and Valentine M. Moghadam. New York: Palgrave Macmillan, 2016. 149-170.

Knibbe, Kim, and Helena Kupari. "Theorizing Lived Religion: Introduction." *Journal of Contemporary Religion* 35:2 (2020): 157-176.

Knibbe, Kim. "Is Critique Possible in the Study of Lived Religion? Anthropological and Feminist Reflections." *Journal of Contemporary Religion* 35.2 (2020): 251-268.

Knott, Kim. "Living Religious Practices." In *Intersections of Religion and Migration -Issues at the Global Crossroads*, edited by Jennifer B. Saunders, Elena Fiddian-Qasmiyeh, and Susanna Snyder. New York: Palgrave Macmillan, 2016. 71-90.

Kokkonen, Outi. "A Faceless Threat or Vulnerable Individuals?: The Representations of Refugees in British Newspapers during the European Refugee Crisis." BA Thesis, University of Jyväskylä, 2017.

Koss-Chioino, Joan D., and Philip Hefner, eds. *Spiritual Transformation and Healing - Anthropological, Theological, Neuroscientific, and Clinical Perspectives*. Oxford: AltaMira, 2006.

Köngeter, Stefan. *Paradoxes of Transnational Knowledge Production in Social Work*. London, New York: Routledge, 2012.

Kumsa, Martha. "'No! I'm Not a Refugee!' The Poetics of Be-longing among Youth Oromos in Toronto." *Journal of Refugee Studies* 19. 2 (2006): 230-255.

Kupari, Helena. "Lived Religion and the Religious Field." *Journal of Contemporary Religion* 35.2 (2020): 213-230.

Kuppinger, Petra. "Lived Religion and Female Informal Authority in a Neighborhood in Stuttgart, Germany." In *Gender and Authority across Disciplines, Space and Time*, edited by Adele Bardazzi and Alberica Bazzoni. Cham: Palgrave Macmillan, 2020. 221-39.

Kvale, Steinar, and Svend Brinkmann. *Interviews: Learning the Craft of Qualitative Research Interviewing*. London, Thousand Oaks, CA: Sage, 2009.

Laban, Cornelis. "Resilience-Oriented Treatment of Traumatised Asylum Seekers and Refugees." In *Trauma and Migration – Cultural Factors in the Diagnosis and Treatment of Traumatised Immigrants*, edited by Meryam Schouler-Ocak. Cham: Springer, 2015. 191-208.

Lauterbach, Karen. "Religion and Displacement in Africa." *Religion and Theology* 21.3 (2014): 290-308.

Levitt, Peggy. "Religion on the Move: Mapping Global Cultural Production and Consumption." In *Religion on the Edge: De-centering and Re-centering the Sociology of Religion*, edited by Courtney Bender, Wendy Cadge, Peggy Levitt, and David Smilde. Oxford: Oxford University Press, 2012. 159-78.

Leydesdorff, Selma. "When All is Lost: Metanarrative in the Oral History of Hanifa, Survivor of Srebrenica." In *Listening on the Edge, Oral History in the Aftermath of Crisis*, edited by Mark Cave and Stephen Sloane. New York: Oxford Oral History Series, 2014. 17-33.

Liebelt, Claudia, and Pnina Werbner. "Gendering 'Everyday Islam': An Introduction." *Contemporary Levant* 3:1(2018): 2-9. DOI: 10.1080/20581831.2018.1449932

López, Javier, Celia Camilli, and Christina Noreiga. "Posttraumatic Growth in Widowed and Non-widowed Older Adults: Religiosity and Sense of Coherence." *Journal of Religion and Health* 54 (2015):1612-1628.

Louw, Maria Elisabeth. *Everyday Islam in Post-Soviet Central Asia*. London. New York: Routledge, 2007.

Lynch, Gordon. *The Sacred in the Modern World – A Cultural Sociological Approach*. Oxford: Oxford University Press, 2012.

Mahajan, Shreya, Samantha B. Meyer, and Elena Neiterman. "Identifying the Impact of Social Networks on Mental and Emotional Health Seeking Behaviours Amongst Women Who are Refugees from Syria Living in Canada." *Global Public Health* (2021) DOI: 10.1080/17441692.2021.1872679

Mahmood, Saba. "Feminist Theory, Agency, and the Liberatory Subject: Some Reflections on the Islamic Revival in Egypt." *Temenos-Nordic Journal of Comparative Religion* 42.1 (2006): 31-71.

Malik, Iftikhar H. *Curating Lived Islam in the Muslim World: British Scholars, Sojourners and Sleuths.* London, New York: Routledge, 2021.

Mandaville, Peter. *Transnational Muslim Politics - Reimagining the Umma.* London, New York: Routledge, 2001.

Manjikian, Lalai. "Refugee 'In-betweenness': A Proactive Existence." *Refuge: Canada's Journal on Refugees* 27.1 (2011): 50-58. https://doi.org/10.25071/1920-7336.34355

Maritato, Chiara. *Women, Religion, and the State in Contemporary Turkey.* Cambridge: Cambridge University Press, 2020.

Mayer, Jean-François. "'In God Have I Put My Trust': Refugees And Religion." *Refugee Survey Quarterly* 26.2 (2007): 6-10.

McAndrew, Siobhan, and David Voas. "Measuring Religiosity Using Surveys." *Survey Question Bank: Topic Overview* 4 (2011) https://ukdataservice.ac.uk/media/263004/discover_sqb_religion_mcandrew_voas.pdf

McDaugall, Ann. "Hidden in the Household: Gender and Class in the Study of Islam in Africa." *CJAS* 42.2-3 (2008): 508-45.

McGuire, Meredith. *Lived Religion – Faith and Practice in Everyday Life.* Oxford: Oxford University Press, 2008.

___. "What Really Matters." *Spiritus: A Journal of Christian Spirituality* 6.1 (2006): 107-12.

___. *Religion: The Social Context.* Belmont, CA: Wadsworth Thomson Learning, 2002.

McMichael, Celia. "Everywhere is Allah's Place: Islam and the Everyday Life of Somali Women in Melbourne, Australia." *Journal of Refugee Studies* 15.2 (2002): 171-188.

Meyer, Birgit. "Mobilizing Theory." In *Refugees and Religion – Ethnographic Studies of Global Trajectories*, edited by Birgit Meyer and Peter van der Veer. New York: Bloomsbury Academic, 2021. 256-273.

Miled, Neila. "Can the Displaced Speak? Muslim Refugee Girls Negotiating Identity, Home and Belonging through Photovoice." *Women's Studies International Forum* 81 (2020) https://doi.org/10.1016/j.wsif.2020.102381

Minh-ha, Trin. *Woman, Native, Other: Writing Postcoloniality and Feminism.* Bloomington: Indiana University Press, 1989.

___. *Elsewhere, Within here. Immigration, Refugeeism, and The Boundary Event.* London: Routledge, 2011.

Moghissi, Haideh, and Halleh Ghorashi (eds). *Muslim Diaspora in the West: Negotiating Gender, Home and Belonging.* New York: Routledge, 2010.

Mohaghegh Harandi, Negin. "Individualized Islamic Practices and Proving 'Normality' - Thoughts and Experiences of Muslim International Students Regarding Their Muslim Identities and Everyday Religious Practices in Swedish Society." MA Thesis, University of Gothenburg, 2019. http://hdl.handle.net/2077/62164

Munt, Sally R. "Journeys of Resilience: The Emotional Geographies of Refugee Women." *Gender, Place & Culture* 19.5 (2012): 555-577.

Murphy, James. "Beyond 'Religion' and 'Spirituality': Extending a 'Meaning Systems' Approach to Explore Lived Religion." *Psychology of Religion* 39:1 (2017): 1-26.

Nathal, Dessing, Nadia Jeldtoft, Jørgen Nielsen, and Linda Woodhead, eds. *Everyday Lived Islam in Europe.* Farnham, Surrey: Ashgate, 2013.

Nasir, Kamaludeen Mohamed. *Globalized Muslim Youth in the Asia Pacific: Popular Culture in Singapore and Sydney.* Hampshire: Palgrave Macmillan, 2016.

Nayel, Amina Alrasheed. *Alternative Performativity of Muslimness -The Intersection of Race, Gender, Religion, and Migration.* London and New York: Palgrave Macmillan, 2017.

Negura, Lilian, Corinna Buhay, Annamaria Silvana de Rosa. "Mirrored Social Representations of Canadian Caseworkers with Migratory Paths Intervening with Refugees in the Host Country." *International Journal of Environmental Research and Public Health* 18:16 (2021): 8648. https://doi.org/10.3390/ijerph18168648

Neitz, Mary Jo. "Feminist Methodologies." In *Routledge Handbook of Research Methods in the Study of Religion*, edited by Michael Stausberg and Steven Engler. London, New York: Routledge, 2011. 54-67.

Neuger, Christie. *Counseling Women: A Narrative, Pastoral Approach*. Minneapolis: Fortress, 2001.

Ngunjiri, Faith Wambura, Katy-Ann C. Hernandez, and Heewon Chang. "Living Autoethnography: Connecting Life and Research [Editorial]." *Journal of Research Practice* 6.1 (2010): 1-17. http://jrp.icaap.org/index.php/jrp/article/view/241/186

Nielsen, Jørgen. *Muslims in Western Europe*. Edinburgh: Edinburgh University Press, 2016.

Nyhagen, Line. "The Lived Religion Approach In The Sociology of Religion and Its Implications for Secular Feminist Analyses of Religion." *Social Compass* 64.4 (2017): 495-511.

Nyhagen, Line, and Beatrice Halsaa, eds. *Religion, Gender and Citizenship – Women of Faith, Gender Equality*. London and New York: Palgrave Macmillan, 2016.

Oakley, Ann. "Interviewing Women Again: Power, Time and the Gift." *Sociology* 50.1 (2016): 195-213.

Olufadi, Yunusa. "Muslim Daily Religiosity Assessment Scale (MUDRAS): A New Instrument for Muslim Religiosity Research and Practice." *Psychology of Religion and Spirituality* 9.2 (2017): 165-179.

Orsi, Robert. "Everyday Religion and the Contemporary World – The Un-Modern, or What Was Supposed to Have Disappeared But Did Not." In *Ordinary Lives and Grand Schemes – An Anthropology of Everyday Religion,* edited by Samuli Schielke and Liza Debevec. New York: Berghahn, 2012. 115-125.

___. Introduction to *The Cambridge Companion to Religious Studies*, edited by Robert Orsi. Cambridge: Cambridge University Press, 2011. 1-13.

___. *The Madonna of 115th Street: Faith and Community in Italian Harlem,* 1880-1950. New Haven, CT: Yale University Press, 2010.

___. "When 2+2=5, Can We Begin to Think about Unexplained Religious Experiences in Ways That Acknowledge Their Existence?" *The American Scholar* 76 (2007): 34-43.

___. *Between Heaven and Earth: The Religious Worlds People Make and The Scholars Who Study Them*. Princeton, N.J.: Princeton University Press, 2005.

___. "Everyday Miracles: The Study of Lived Religion." In *Lived Religion in America: Toward a History of Practice*, edited by David D. Hall. Princeton, N.J.: Princeton University Press, 1997. 3-21.

Ossman, Susan. *Shifting Worlds, Shaping Fieldwork: A Memoir of Anthropology and Art*. London, New York: Routledge, 2021.

___. *Moving Matters: Paths of Serial Migration*. Palo Alto: Stanford UP, 2013.

Otto, Rudolf. *The Idea of the Holy. An Inquiry into the Non-Rational Factor in the Idea of the Divine and Its Relation to the Rational*. London: Oxford University Press, 1936.

Österlind, Leila Karin, and Pia Karlsson Minganti. "New Faces of a New Phase: The Politics of Visibility Among Young Muslim Women in Sweden." In *New Dimensions of Diversity in Nordic Culture and Society*, edited by Jenny Björklund and Ursula Lindqvist. Newcastle upon Tyne: Cambridge Scholars Publishing, 2016. 41-60.

Pargament, Kenneth. *The Psychology of Religion and Coping - Theory, Research, Practice*. New York: Guilford Press, 1997.

___. "The Meaning of Spiritual Transformation." In *Spiritual Transformation and Healing - Anthropological, Theological, Neuroscientific, and Clinical Perspectives*, edited by Joan D Koss-Chioino and Philip Hefner. Oxford: AltaMira, 2006. 10-24.

___. *Spiritually Integrated Psychotherapy: Understanding and Addressing the Sacred*. New York: Guilford, 2007.

Peter, Frank. "Individualization and Religious Authority in Western European Islam." *Islam and Christian-Muslim Relations* 17.1 (2006): 105-118.

Philipps, Anne, Fran Porter, and Nicola Slee, eds. *Researching Female Faith - Qualitative Research Methods*. London, New York: Routledge, 2018.

Predelli, Line Nyhagen. "Interpreting Gender in Islam. A Case Study of Immigrant Muslim Women in Oslo, Norway." *Gender & Society* 18.4 (2004): 473–493.

Ramadhan, Riskiansyah. "Securitization of Islam: A Case of Muslims in Cyprus." *Academic Journal of Islamic Studies* 5.2 (2020): 179-196.

Reinhart, Kevin. *Lived Islam – Colloquial Religion in a Cosmopolitan Tradition*. Cambridge: Cambridge University Press, 2020.

Robbins, Joel. "What is the Matter with Transcendence? On the Place of Religion in the New Anthropology of Ethics." *Journal of the Royal Anthropological Institute* 22 (2016): 767-808.

___. "Anthropology and Theology: An Awkward Relationship?" *Anthropological Quarterly* 79. 2 (2006): 285-94.

Rokib, Mohammad, and Syamsul Sodiq. "Muslims with Tattoos: The Punk Muslim Community in Indonesia." *Journal of Islamic Studies* 55.1 (2017): 47-70.

Ruokonen-Engler, Minna-Kristiina, and Irini Siouti. "Doing Biographical Reflexivity as a Methodological Tool in Transnational Research Settings." *Transnational Social Review* 3.2 (2014): 247-261.

Salam, Muhammad Talha, Nazlida Muhamad, and Vai Shiem Leong. "Measuring Religiosity among Muslim Consumers: Observations and Recommendations." *Journal of Islamic Marketing* 10.2 (2019): 633-652.

Salih, Ruba. "Bodies That Walk, Bodies That Talk, Bodies That Love: Palestinian Women Refugees, Affectivity, and the Politics of the Ordinary." *Antipode* 49.3 (2017): 742-760.

Sartre, Jean-Paul. *Search for a Method*. Translated by Hazel E. Barns. New York: Vintage Books, 1968.

Saunders, Jennifer, Elena Fiddian-Qasmiyeh, and Susanna Snyder, eds. *Intersections of Religion and Migration: Issues at the Global Crossroads*. New York: Springer, 2016.

Schielke, Samuli, and Liza Debevec, eds. *Ordinary Lives and Grand Schemes – An Anthropology of Everyday Religion*. New York: Berghahn, 2012.

Schmiedel, Ulrich, and Graeme Smith, eds. *Religion in the European Refugee Crisis*. London: Palgrave Macmillan, 2018.

Schmoller, Jesko. "The Talking Dead: Everyday Muslim Practice in Russia." Special Issue on Everyday Nationalism in World Politics. *Nationalities Papers* 48.6 (2020): 1036-1051.

Schreiter, Robert. "Spaces for Religion and Migrants Religious Identity." *Forum Mission* 5 (2009): 155-171.

Shakman Hurd, Elizabeth. *Beyond Religious Freedom – The New Global Politics of Religion*. Princeton and Oxford: Princeton University Press, 2015.

Shalaby, Nadia. "Positioning in the Oral Narratives of Displaced Syrian Women." *Journal of Refugee Studies* 32. 3 (2018): 456-480.

Shaw, Annick, and Stephen Joseph. "Religion, Spirituality, and Posttraumatic Growth: A Systematic Review." *Mental Health, Religion and Culture* 8:1 (2005): 1-11.

Shaw, Stacey, Laurel Peacock, Latifa Ali, Veena Pillai, and Altaf Husain. "Religious Coping and Challenges Among Displaced Muslim Female Refugees." *Affilia* 34: 4 (2019): 518-534.

Sheftel, Anna. "Talking and Not Talking about Violence: Challenges in Interviewing Survivors of Atrocity as Whole People." *Oral History Review* 2 (2018): 288-303.

Shobhana Xavier, Merin. "Gendering the Divine: Women, Femininity, and Queer Identities on the Sufi Path." In *The Routledge Handbook of Islam and Gender*, edited by Justine Howe. London, New York: Routledge, 2021.

Silvestri, Sara. "Faith intersections and Muslim Women in the European Microcosm: Notes towards the Study of Non-organized Islam." *Ethnic and Racial Studies* 34.7 (2011): 1230-1247.

___. "Comparing Burqa Debates in Europe: Sartorial Styles, Religious Prescriptions and Political Ideologies," In *Religion in Public Spaces,* edited by Silvio Ferrari and Sabrina

Pastorelli. Farnham, Surrey: Ashgate, 2012. 275-94.

___. "Misperceptions of the 'Muslim Diaspora'." *Current History* 115.784 (2016): 319-321.

Simich, Laura, and Lisa Andermann, eds. *Refugee and Resilience - Promoting Resilience and Mental Health among Resettled Refugees and Forced Migrants*. New York: Springer, 2014.

Simmel, Georg. *Essays on Religion*. New Haven: Yale University Press, 1997.

Simsir, Zeynep, and Bulent Dilmac. "Predictive Relationship Between War Posttraumatic Growth, Values, and Perceived Social Support." *Illness, Crisis and Loss* (2018): 1-17.

Sink, Alys. "The Role of Refugee Women Narratives in the U.S. Resettlement Process." MA Thesis, James Madison University, 2017.

Sleep, Lenora. "Personal Encounters with Sociology, Religion, and Issues of Gender." *Sociology of Religion* 61.4 (2000): 473-477.

Smith, Kate. "Stories Told By, For, and About Women Refugees: Engendering Resistance." *International Journal for Critical Geographies* 14.2 (2015): 461-69.

Smith, Wilfred Cantwell. *The Meaning and End of Religion*. London: SPCK, 1978.

Soelle, Dorothee. *The Silent Cry: Mysticism and Resistance*. Translated by Barbara Rumscheidt and Martin Rumscheidt. Minneapolis: Fortress, 2001.

Sointu, Eeva, and Linda Woodhead. "Spirituality, Gender, and Expressive Selfhood." *Journal for the Scientific Study of Religion* 47.2 (2008): 259-276.

Spahić Šiljak, Zilka. *Shining Humanity: Life Stories of Women in Bosnia and Herzegovina*. Newcastle upon Tyne: Cambridge Scholars Publishing, 2014.

___, ed. *Contesting Female, Feminist and Muslim Identities - Post-Socialist Contexts of Bosnia and Herzegovina and Kosovo*. Sarajevo: Center for Interdisciplinary Postgraduate Studies, 2012.

Sprague, Joey. *Feminist Methodologies for Critical Researchers -Bridging Differences*. Walnut Creek, CA: Alta Mira, 2005.

Sremac, Srdjan, and Ines W. Jindra. "Negotiating of Self, the Social, and the Sacred in Recovery: A Lived Religion Perspective." In *Lived Religion, Conversion and Recovery: Negotiating of Self, the Social and the Sacred*, edited by Srdjan Sremac and Ines W. Jindra. London and New York: Palgrave Macmillan, 2020. 1-12.

Sremac, Srdjan, and R. Ruard Ganzevoort, eds. *Trauma and Lived Religion - Transcending the Ordinary*. London and New York: Palgrave, 2018.

___. "Lived Religion and Lived (In)Tolerance." In *Lived Religion and the Politics of (In)Tolerance*, edited by R. Ruard Ganzevoort and Srdjan Sremac. London and New York: Palgrave, 2017. 1-15.

Stanley, Liz. *Feminist Praxis: Research, Theory and Epistemology in Feminist Sociology*. London, New York: Routledge, 1990.

Streib, Heinz, Astrid Dinter, and Kerstin Söderblom, eds. *Lived Religion - Conceptual, Empirical and Practical-Theological Approaches*. Leiden, Boston: Brill, 2008.

Streib, Heinz. "More Spiritual Than Religious: Changes In The Religious Field Require New Approaches." In *Lived Religion – Conceptual, Empirical and Practical-Theological Approaches*, edited by Heinz Streib, Astrid Dinter, and Kerstin Söderblom. Leiden, Boston: Brill, 2008. 53-67.

Stringer, Martin D. "The Sounds of Silence: Searching for the Religious in Everyday Discourse." In *Social Identities between the Sacred and the Secular*, edited by Abby Day, Giselle Vincett, and Christopher R. Cotter. Burlington, VT: Ashgate, 2013. 161–71.

Sutherland, Cheryl, and Yang Cheng. "Participatory-action Research with (im)migrant Women in Two Small Canadian Cities: Using Photovoice in Kingston and Peterborough, Ontario." *Journal of Immigrant and Refugee Studies* 7.3 (2009): 290-307.

Taysom, Stephen. "Abundant Events or Narrative Abundance: Robert Orsi and the Academic Study of Mormonism." *Dialogue: A Journal of Mormon Thought* 45.4 (2012):1-26.

Tedeschi, Richard, and Lawrence Calhoun. *Trauma and Transformation: Growing in the Aftermath of Suffering*. Thousand Oaks, CA: Sage, 1995.

Tedeschi, Richard, Arnie Cann, Kanako Taku, Emre Senol-Durak, and Lawrence Calhoun. "The Posttraumatic Growth Inventory: A Revision Integrating Existential and Spiritual Change." *Journal of Traumatic Stress* 30 (2017): 11-18.

The Pew Forum. "Faith on the Move -The Religious Affiliation of International Migrants."
https://www.pewforum.org/2012/03/08/religious-migration-exec/

Tobin, Sarah A. "Modelling Exile - Syrian Women Gather to Discuss Prophetic Examples in Jordan." In *The Routledge Handbook of Islam and Gender*, edited by Justine Howe. New York: Routledge, 2021. 282-296.

Trinka, Eric, M. "Migration and Internal Religious Pluralism: A Review of Present Findings." *The Journal of Interreligious Studies* 28 (2019a): 3-23.

___. "Religion on the Move: Mobility, Migration and Internal Religious: Diversity in Biblical and Early Israel and Judah." *Revista do Museu de Arqueologia e Etnologia* 33 (2019b): 66-90.

___. "Mirrored Selves: Reflections on Religious Narrative (s) in the Lives of Migrants." In *Handbook of Culture and Migration*, edited by Jeffrey H. Cohen and Ibrahim Sirkeci. Cheltenham, UK: Elgar, 2021. 68–81.

___. "Re: from the Intro/literature review section of my book." Received by Ozlem Ezer. February 16, 2021.

Turaeva, Rano. "Imagined Mosque Communities in Russia: Central Asian Migrants in Moscow." *Asian Ethnicity* 20.2 (2019):131-147.

Van der Veer, Peter. "Introduction: Refugees and Religion." In *Refugees and Religion – Ethnographic Studies of Global Trajectories*, edited by Birgit Meyer and Peter van der Veer. New York: Bloomsbury Academic, 2021.1-11.

Van Dijk, Teun. *Ideology: A Multidisciplinary Approach*. London: Sage Publications, 1998.

Vicini, Fabio. "Lived Islam in post-Soviet Russia: Officials, Experts, and Ordinary Interpretations of Islam." *Ethnicities* 20.4 (2020).

Vidmar Horvat, Ksenija. "Visualisation of the 'Balkan road': Media Representations of the Refugee Crisis at the Periphery of Europe." *Culture, Practice and Europeanization* 5.1 (2020): 67-84.

Vinding, Niels Valdemar. "Churchification of Islam in Europe." In *Exploring the Multitude of Muslims in Europe - Essays in Honour of Jørgen S. Nielsen*, edited by Niels Valdemar Vinding, Egdunas Racius, and Jörn Thielmann. Leiden: Brill, 2018. 50-66.

Vuola, Elina. "Intersectionality in Latin America? The possibilities of Intersectional Analysis in Latin American Studies and Study of Religion." In *Bodies and Borders in Latin America*, edited by Silje Lundgren, Thaïs Machado-Borges, and Charlotta Widmark. Stockholm: Institute of Latin American Studies, Stockholm University, 2012. 131-151.

___. "Feminist Theology, Religious Studies and Gender Studies: Mutual Challenges." In *Contemporary Encounters in Gender and Religion - European Perspectives,* edited by Lena Gemzöe, Marja-Liisa Keinänen, and Avril Maddrell. London: Palgrave, 2016. 307-34.

Walker, Peter, Dyan Mazurana, Amy Warren, George Scarlett, and Henry Louis. "The Role of Spirituality in Humanitarian Crisis Survival and Recovery." In *Sacred Aid: Faith and Humanitarianism,* edited by Michael Barnett and Janice Stein. Oxford: Oxford University Press, 2012. 115-139.

Walton, Heather. *Writing Methods in Theological Reflection*. London: SCM Press, 2014.

Walczak, Bartłomiej, and Nikolaos Lampas. "Beliefs on Refugees as a Terrorist Threat. The Social Determinants of Refugee-related Stereotypes." *Studia Migracyjne-Przegląd Polonijny* 176 (2020): 53-70.

Whitehead, Amy. 2020. "A Method of 'Things'": A Relational Theory of Objects as Persons in Lived Religious Practice." *Journal of Contemporary Religion* 35 (2): 231–250.

Yalouri, Eleana. "Difficult Representations. Visual Art Engaging with the Refugee Crisis." *Visual Studies* 34. 3 (2019): 223-238.

Yandell, Keith. *Philosophy of Religion: A Contemporary Introduction*. London, New York: Routledge, 1999.

Zaman, Tahir. "What's Faith got to do with it?" *Forced Migration Review* 48 (2014): 84.

Zarkov, Dubravka. "Reflecting on Faith and Feminism." *European Journal of Women's Studies* 22.1 (2015): 3–6.

www.ingramcontent.com/pod-product-compliance
Lightning Source LLC
Chambersburg PA
CBHW071748270326
41928CB00013B/2838